Escaping The Iron Cage

Making The Workplace Suitable For Humans

By
Patrick B. Sullivan

First edition: 2026

ISBNs:

eBook: 979-8-29583-819-4
Paperback: 979-8-90321-076-3
Hardcover: 979-8-90321-077-0

Published by: David McKay Publications
Printed in: United States of America

For permission requests, contact:
sabrina@davidmckaypublication.com

Table of Contents

Dedication

This book is dedicated to every person who comes home from work pissed off!

Acknowledgement

This book would not be possible without the support of so many people. I am grateful to my family, especially my children and grandchildren who encouraged me to write down what I have learned over the years. My brother and sister were very patient with me as I rambled on about what I was writing. It is so important to have a "sounding board" when putting together my thoughts and ideas. I have friends who served that role so very well. I especially want to acknowledge the vital role played by my friend, Joe Schopfer, with whom I have had so many constructive conversations. One of the great challenges in writing is to push through to the end. My friend, Dale Joslyn, helped me as I entered the final lap.

Of course, none of this would be possible without the various mentors and teachers I have had. My thought processes were opened incredibly by the faculty of the University of Southern California School of Public Administration. My confidence was fostered by the faculty and staff of the University of Montana. I was encouraged and challenged by Commander McCaw and my friend Tom Calvin while I was in the Navy. They instilled in me the belief that I could succeed in advancing my education. It may seem that I have had only terrible supervisors over the years. However, that is not true. I was inspired by many of my leaders. I grew as a professional under the guidance of President Don Kettner, who modeled what an effective leader should look like.

Introduction

"We have to work together, but we don't have to be friends." I have heard this statement or some variation of it many times. It is one of those adages we encounter regularly that we accept as a truism. I heard it several times during my interviews with employees of a team that had long-term problems with conflict. On this day, however, it struck me that this accepted truth is wrong. I have just completed my tenth interview with employees in a team of nineteen. This was part of a consultation to help the team that was mired in conflict. Every one of the interviewees proffered this remark during our conversation. It is something that is said so frequently that I usually do not include it in my notes. I did this time and the subsequent nine times that followed. Every single member of the team uttered this concept. In fact, the managers said something similar when I first met with them. This was the "red flag" I was looking for as a hook for helping the team develop solutions. Why was it so important to offer this remark? This is a key to understand-ding organizational culture. From this point, I realized that this premise was a key indicator of the trouble with how we organize.

A little backstory is necessary here. I have been hired numerous times as a consultant to help teams deal with morale or conflict issues. Typically, I can discover the root of the problem and then facilitate a process where the team can develop solutions. Unfortunately, the solutions didn't always stick. After a period of peace and cooperation, the group begins to backslide into conflict and low morale. There was something about this case that drew my attention to a possible cause. I remember getting the call from one of the managers asking for help. She described her situation that appeared to go through repeated cycles. The conflict regularly built to a crescendo that resulted in people quitting or refusing to work with others. The manager(s) then called a meeting of the whole team to hash out the difficulties. This would result in a new period of peace.

Unfortunately, the tensions would return a few months later, resulting in the same process. This had been going on for seven years.

My sense was that the meetings were not getting to the root cause(s) of the conflict. This is generally the case because the discussions in such meetings don't ordinarily get to the bottom of things. There are a few reasons for this that are evident. One problem is that there are too many possible relationships involved. One of the most important principles of conflict resolution is that one needs to get to the key dyads or one-on-one conflicts. Often, the conflict begins with two people. Over time, alliances form around the initial conflict. Unless the group can identify the initial cause, the underlying issues will just continue to simmer. The group meeting usually only deals with symptoms.

Another problem with group process for conflict is that there are almost always people who do not speak up. Consequently, there are issues that go unidentified. Even though the non-participants choose to keep quiet, they will still harbor resentment. Naturally, this resentment will sow the seeds of future conflict. A related reason the group resolutions don't take is that meetings can be chaotic. It doesn't take long before the frustration of the process leads to quick solutions. These focus on symptoms. What appears to be consent is just surrender.Knowing that team meetings rarely resolve issues, especially those that require a consultant, the process I use is to begin with one-on-one meetings with every team member. These interviews take an hour to an hour-and-a-half. During the interview, I listened for key factors. The first are the relational messages. All messages include both a content level and a relational level. For example, the content might be about the copy machine. That is rarely the cause of conflict. The relational level might be whether one person should be "calling out" another for the purpose of using the copy machine. This is the actual root cause. I will develop this further in a later chapter.

For some reason, on this day, in the middle of nineteen interviews, the adage about not having to be friends caught my attention. Here I was listening for relational messages, and I was missing the meta-perspective. The truth of the matter is that they were not engaging in relationship-building. This was intentional. The group members operated on the belief that they did not need to do this. The underlying belief is that people have their personal lives and their professional lives. These should be kept separate. We really believe that our work is not personal. Consequently, a work colleague or superior (terms I will deal with later) can begin feedback with "don't take this personally…" Everyone knows what word comes next – "but…" The problem here is that our work is personal. Like it or not, work is a form of human expression. When we produce something or solve a problem, it is a personal accomplishment. To expect a person not to take criticism of their work personally is ludicrous.

We spend the largest blocks of time with our work colleagues. Why would anyone conclude that these relationships don't require the same level of effort as our other relationships? It really doesn't make sense. The idea of organizing is to take full advantage of collective effort. The only way we can do that is to get to know one another. This especially includes learning about each other's strengths. We don't all have the same strengths, and that is a good thing. The best outcomes occur when the assets of everyone are allowed to come out. This will not happen on its own. We need to learn what talents are available and apply them. The best athletic coaches are those who have a talent for identifying strengths and using the best combination of team members to achieve success. They also build a team that trusts each other to do their part. This is no different for work teams. Trust does not come about on its own. It requires considerable effort and, more importantly, risk.

The belief that we don't need to be friends in the workplace is partly vested in both our pragmatic and individualist philosophies. As pragmatists, we believe that if something works, it is good. This is easily observed with our acceptance of the adage, "if it ain't broke, don't fix it." The assumption of something not being broken is our "go-to" place. The question is how we determine that something is broken. Generally, it is easy to see that the path of least resistance is to assume something is working. Consequently, if we believe the premise of not needing to be friends in the workplace is working, we won't change it. This may well be because we really haven't known much else. The role played by individualism is fairly obvious. The idea that all value and accomplishment is vested in the individual encourages us to believe that each person will be the creator of their own success (and failures). Self-reliance is a compelling value in our culture, which is reflected in our organizations. However, I can say without reservation, there is no such thing as the "self-made man." The two prevailing philosophies of pragmatism and individualism may have served us well in the past. This is no longer the case. We are now dealing with wicked problems that require better teamwork and stronger networks.

In my previous book, *Rational Gridlock*,[1] I suggested that we create many problems for ourselves by relying on Rationalism. Briefly, Rationalism is the belief that we can solve problems ideally by relying on empirical processes. This is a method that isolates particular variables and tests them for cause-and-effect relationships. The resulting knowledge is then used to develop standard operating procedures. Thus, the people in the organization only need to follow those procedures for a consistent result. Some may contend that we don't do that anymore. However, I believe that it remains quite prevalent. How many articles and conferences are centered around the idea of "best practices" does it take to realize that this relies on the Rational model? Someone tries a process, and it works well. So, then it can be adopted by others for similar results.

---

[1] I wrote this book under my previous name, Patrick B. Edgar. I legally changed my name back to my birth name in 2017

Furthermore, we still rely heavily on the bureaucratic model to organize. This 19th-century creation is premised on Rationality. It is not a stretch to see that bureaucracy is not about people. Max Weber even acknowledges this in his essay *On Bureaucracy*. The model is about positions, not people. He even calls it "the iron cage of rationality." Whenever I bring this up in groups, there is always someone who says we need the chain of command and other features of bureaucracy. We don't have to go very far to see how we got to a point where relationships are viewed as inconvenient. If the system remains impersonal, then all those human passions won't get in the way of accomplishment. Bureaucracy is dehumanizing on many levels. It tends to take the human out of organizations and their relationship with their clients and each other.

Finally, the belief that we can operate in organizations in an impersonal manner arises from a form of self-deception. According to Terry Warner, this is a matter of a psychologistic mindset. People perceive that they must rely on defense mechanisms in society, including organizations. The general belief is that it is vital that we are prepared to defend ourselves from those around us. Since the world is so competitive, we need to watch out for colleagues who might be takers or users. Consequently, one of the most common responses to those around us is offense-taking. This is where we tend to assume that statements or actions that are open to interpretation are more likely to be negative or offensive. Without effective relationship-building, such a response makes the most sense. Most of us have had an experience where we have been in a conflict, only to find out later that there really wasn't a disagreement in the beginning. It is a matter of offense-taking that created the conflict. All of this is tied to the predominance of negativity. We are hard-wired to view things negatively, including ourselves. I will expand on this later.

The following chapters will develop the ideas behind our negativity in terms of dysfunctional organizations. It seems that throughout my career, I have managed to work for all of them or been exposed to them. The first chapter will describe the concept of dysfunction and the attributes that sustain it. The attributes are:

- No relationship-building.
- Arrogance.
- Lack of trust.
- Lack of transparency.
- Control freaks.
- Untrained supervision.

The subsequent chapters expand on each of the attributes. Chapter 2 continues the discussion of no relationship building. Naturally, the first attribute is this lack of relationship-building. Chapter 3 will explore the idea of arrogance. This is not just in terms of individual behavior, but the tendency for the organization to conduct itself with an air of superiority over its own clients or customers. Chapter 4 is dedicated to the lack of trust. I will attempt to describe its source and consequences. Chapter 5 examines the lack of transparency. This is not just a matter of management not being transparent in their decision -making but the common practice of individual team members withholding information as a matter of self-preservation. Chapter 6 will consider the common presence of control freaks. This is directly related to the belief in bureaucracy. It will examine the phenomenon of untrained supervisors. This is a long-standing problem in our organizations. Somehow, we believe that there are born leaders or that this is not a skill that needs to be taught. Consequently, there is little progress in terms of improving organizational culture. Chapter 8 examines further the principles of bureaucracy, especially in terms of its pathology. Chapter 9 addresses a key source of our dysfunctions, our education system. From the beginning in K-12 systems through higher education, we are not prepared to operate in effective human organizations. The following chapters offer some alternative strategies for overcoming these dysfunctions. Chapter 10 considers the changing nature of organizations in the Twenty-First Century. The reality is that postmodern organizations deal with very different challenges. We cannot use industrial structures and methods to address these challenges. Chapter 11 emphasizes the different types of leadership. It also expands the principles to apply to followership. There is no leading without following. Chapter 12 begins the discussion of a combination of principles that I identify as the authentic triangle, composed of authentic leadership, second-wave positive psychology, and mindfulness, beginning with authentic leadership. Chapter 13 presents the principles of positive psychology (specifically, on what is called "second wave positive psychology.") Chapter 14 develops the practices associated with mindfulness. Finally, Chapter 15 presents a call to relational leadership. More specifically, it insists that we must finally move on from the Rational model, building on it to a more humanistic way of thinking. It will do no good to attempt more progressive organizational functioning if we don't embrace the paradigm shift that is crucial. The physical sciences have moved on from the rational paradigm to include quantum dynamics and chaos theory. It is time for the social sciences to do likewise. Every person in our organization has a certain responsibility to take on a leadership role in relationship-building. It is time to discard the notion that "we have to work together, but we don't have to be friends."

Chapter 1:
Dysfunctional Organizations

The Merriam-Webster Dictionary defines dysfunctional as "1. Not functioning properly: marked by impaired or abnormal functioning: 2. Characterized by abnormal or unhealthy interpersonal behavior or interaction." In the context of organizations, the meaning is exactly the same. According to Angela Montgomery:

The word dysfunctional contains the prefix dys- from the Greek meaning 'bad,' 'abnormal,' difficult,' or 'impaired.' We can say that an organization is dysfunctional when it works in a way that is *not consistent with the goal* it's supposed to pursue.

Why would that happen? Because there is a lack of clarity and understanding of the goal. This could easily produce dysfunctional behaviour, meaning behavior that's not consistent with that goal. Very often, what could be perceived as dysfunctional toward a stated goal can be extremely functional for a non-verbalized one. (Montgomery, 2016)

We need to consider what the goal is for organizations. Typically, goals in organizations are stated in terms of some kind of product or service. That makes sense, of course. However, there is another goal that is overlooked. We organize to take advantage of collective efforts. This is not just a matter of the sum of the parts, i.e., the people. One should assume by using the term "organization" itself that we intend for there to be even more. Another way of describing what should happen is teamwork. What do we usually visualize when we think of a team? A common image we use is with a sports team. The successful team is one that wins games. This is accomplished by everyone knowing their role and supporting each other. In fact, when you have a team of individuals who only look after their own success, the group rarely wins. We have seen this many times. In the professional sports realm, there are many instances where the best players are recruited, and the team flops.

So, why is it that these teams fail? If a team had the best players, they would get the best results. That would only be if the best possible outcome is just a sum of their talents. The main reason for such poor results is that they are not teams; they are merely groups. Teams don't happen just because a collection of players is put together under the same label. They happen because the leadership works to get the players to trust and support each other. Further, the manager makes sure that the players' strengths are used to the best possible outcomes. Without that level of coordination and relationship-building, there will be no or little success. The same principles apply to all organizations to some extent. Even in cases where the members work independently, there still needs to be relationship-building and coordination. That's why it is called "teamwork" and not "groupwork."

In my experience, I have found that there are seven main factors that lead to a dysfunctional organization. They may not be the only ones, but I have noticed these as the most common.

They are:

Lack of relationship-building.

Arrogance.

Lack of trust.

Lack of transparency.

Excessive emphasis on control.

Undeveloped leaders.

Poor conflict skills.

These issues naturally overlap and contribute to one another. However, I am laying them out separately to create a clearer picture.

I recognize there are tens of thousands of books on organizations and leadership. There is a wealth of great information out there. I humbly submit that there are a couple of elements that are missing. The first one is the lack of relationship-building. The second is essentially the source of these failures. As I described in my previous book, *Rational Gridlock*, our continued commitment to the Rational model is the driving force that keeps us trapped in these dysfunctions. I hope to make this case through a combination of the evidence found in the literature and through my own experiences as case studies. I have thought about this for the past fifty years and believe I have found the root of the challenges we find in organizations and the culture at large. The foundation of the difficulties lies in the perception that organizations are not made up of people. That may sound a little strange, but it is intentional. Frederick Taylor set the stage with his Scientific Management (Taylor, The Principles of Scientific Management, 1911), which is premised on the Rational model. The main idea is to manage the workers based on scientific principles of efficiency. There is one best way to perform tasks, and it is discoverable through structured observation. This is the very essence of the empirical method that is the basis of the Rational model. The idea was to eliminate the individual creativity of labor. By extension, this replaces the human spirit with a mechanistic one.

The classic presentation of the application of the Rational model to organizations is proffered by Max Weber in his *Essays in Sociology*. (Weber, Bureaucracy, 1946) In his essay, "Bureaucracy," Weber lays out the clear principles of how modern organizations function. The principles he lays out are as follows:

There is a principle of fixed and official jurisdictional areas, which are generally ordered by rules, that is, by laws or administrative regulations.

The principles of office hierarchy and of levels of graded authority mean a firmly ordered system of super- and subordination in which there is a supervision of the lower offices by the higher ones.

The management of the modern office is based upon written documents ("the files"), which are preserved in their original or draught form.

Office management, at least all specialized office management—and such management is distinctly modern—usually presupposes thorough and expert training.

When the office is fully developed, official activity demands the full working capacity of the official, irrespective of the fact that his obligatory time in the bureau may be firmly delimited.

The management of the office follows general rules, which are more or less stable, more or less exhaustive, and which can be learned. (Weber, Bureaucracy, 1946)

Notice what is missing in this description—people. He speaks of offices or positions but not people. This is essential in rational thought. The intention is to prevent the "passions" of humans from interfering with the efficient operation of the organization. He goes further with this by describing the position of the official:

Office-holding is a "vocation." This is shown, first, in the requirement of a firmly prescribed course of training… Furthermore, the position of the official is in the nature of a duty. *This determines the internal structure of his relations,* in the following manner: Legally and actually, office holding is not considered a source to be exploited… [italics added].

The personal position of the official is patterned in the following way: Whether he is in a private office or a public bureau, the modern official always strives and usually enjoys a distinct social esteem as compared with the governed. (Weber, Bureaucracy, 1946).

Again, this does not speak of the person but the office, even defining how relationships are to be conducted.

Many may argue that this is just old stuff. We have come a long way from these antiquated ideas. I do not believe that we have. We may have tweaked these ideas a bit, but the core ideas remain. One of the first reactions I get whenever I talk about flatter organizations or emphasizing trust is, "But we need the hierarchy and control." It is such a firmly established concept that, to many, it is unthinkable to replace it.

To make this point further, we can look at the main organizational theories of the past century. The first modification came in the form of human relations theory (ironically.) The premise was that organizations are social environments. This was prompted by discoveries made during the Hawthorne studies. Briefly, the Hawthorne studies were conducted in the Hawthorne plant of Western Electric between 1927 and 1932. The researchers were interested in the impact of changing the lighting in the plant. However, what happened was that production went up no matter what they did to the lighting. This was at first thought to be a failed experiment. However, Elton Mayo had other ideas. He noted that one of the features of the study was to ask the workers how they felt about the working environment. He contended that this reflected them being treated as people. The studies then continued with various adjustments to the working environment. The results were essentially the same; production went up. This led to suggestions of a more "people-centered" management style. The results were encouragement of various social activities (Smith J. H., 1987). At this point, one might say that the idea of workers not being people was overcome. However, that is not the case. Instead, the reforms that came about were primarily tied to the ideas of efficiency and the manipulation of employees. In other words, there was one best way to manage social relationships.

Another key figure in the Human Resources movement was Abraham Maslow, who posited the hierarchy of needs. (Maslow, A Theory of Human Motivation, 1943) In this construct, Maslow suggested that human beings, especially in organizations, operate under a system of prioritizing their needs. Not everyone has the same priorities, but they are generally in this order. The key theme is that individuals have a prioritization of needs that may vary somewhat but follow a general pattern. The hierarchy is divided into deficiency needs and growth needs. The deficiency needs included: physiological, safety/security, and social needs (some place social needs in the growth area, but I find that they are more basic than that). The growth needs are self-esteem and self-actualization. Later, Maslow expanded the hierarchy to include cognitive, aesthetic, and transcendent. The main consideration here is human motivation. Once again, this concept was used to standardize human behavior and control it by creating incentive systems.

There have been multiple reform movements since the Hawthorne studies. In the 1970s, there was a great deal of interest in the importance of goal setting for the organization and its workers. This is sometimes referred to as the Human Resources movement. The idea was that human beings were at their best when they set goals. (Miles, 1965) "These resources include not only physical skills and energy, but also creative ability and the capacity for responsible, self-directed, self-controlled behavior." (Miles, 1965, 150) Maxwell Maltz described human beings as "goal-striving mechanisms" (Maltz, 1960). Another concept was to apply the principles of social systems theory to organizations. This idea was that organizations are open social systems that must interact with their environments to survive. (Katz, 1966) This approach identifies organizational behavior in terms of input, throughput, output, and feedback loops. Two key features of systems theory are the emphasis on the feedback loop and a longer-term view than that of

Human Resources theory. Unfortunately, it also considers the people in the organization as part of the input.

The modern and postmodern understanding of organizations focuses more on ideas that emerge from reflexive organizational sociology. (Caron, 2013) That is, research that is most effective is more qualitative and relies on personal observation and interviews. Consequently, the more important considerations stem from the interactions between participants. Herbert Simon, for example, focused on decision-making in organizations. He noted that since human beings must operate within what he called "bounded rationality," decisions needed to be made based on what is effective and not optimal. (Simon, Administrative Behavior: A Study of Decision-Making Processes in Administrative Organization, second edition, 1957) Karl Weick emphasized the process of "sense-making" within organizations. The use of information is such that the people within the team develop their own sense of language and meaning. (Weick K. S., 2005) Sometimes, this concentrates on the processes within the establishment, including variation between subunits. This is admittedly about the people, but more about how they attach meaning. I do not see this as much as establishing relationships. It is more about the functioning of the organization.

There is a great deal written recently about organizations that focus on leadership. This is a refreshing development because it stresses the need to move away from management toward leadership. This does become more about people in the relational sense. I will come back to this later, but suffice it to say, we need more about interpersonal relationships. The bottom line (so to speak) is to finally dispense with the Rational underpinnings of how we understand organizations. It is worth noting that the Rational mentality is different, depending on the culture, but has the same result. In North America, the primary form is pragmatism, whereas in other countries it is more likely to be logical positivism. The pragmatic thought is summed up in the notion that "if it works, it's good." The more popular adage is, "if it ain't broke, don't fix it." The alternative in logical positivism is that if all the logic is in place and makes sense, it leads to a decision. The problem with pragmatism is that the definition of "it works" is rather subjective, and the notion of goodness is also debatable. The difficulty with logical positivism is that there is an assumption that sufficient information is available to be confident that the logic is sound. Besides, like it or not, organizations involve people. We also need to dispel the idea that we are rational beings. We are not. We are emotional beings and relational beings, which is a good thing. We also need to be much more comfortable with the reality of our uniqueness. This is a crucial aspect of working together. I will develop this more in the next chapter. The following chapters will focus on each of the attributes of dysfunctional organizations.

In addition to the dominance of the Rational model, we have another compelling influence on organizational behavior that contributes to dysfunction. That is our continued attachment to individualism. (Bengtsson, 1997) One piece of evidence that shows this clearly is the use of the phrase "self-made man." I see this frequently in ads and political rhetoric. The fact is that there is no such thing. Whenever I hear someone making such a claim, I cannot trust them. It suggests that they have no appreciation for their parents, teachers, and mentors in their lives. It also suggests that they fail to appreciate the other people who work in their organization. They also fail to recognize the infrastructure that allows them to operate their business, which is paid for by the community. This conveys the idea that we are all independent agents in terms of how we manage to survive. It also results in people believing that they need to only rely on themselves wherever they work. This is such an unfortunate belief system.

In North America, there is a more robust form of this in rugged individualism. This developed out of the frontier experience, especially in the 19th century. (Samuel Bazzi, 2020) The western areas attracted a certain kind of self-sufficient individual. Of course, it makes sense that such a person would be drawn to settle in the West. There were no services available, and it was incumbent on the settler to provide for his (it was disproportionately males) defense and financial well-being. The resulting culture is one that believes in reliance on one's own efforts to succeed. It also resists any kind of government intervention, especially as it relates to the distribution of wealth. The truth is that this did not remain confined to the frontier experience. Rather, the image of the rugged individual was preserved in literature and other media.

Consequently, it is deeply embedded in the culture to this day. This carries over into our organizations. Just a quick review of the general characteristics of how people view their work experiences reveals this philosophy. The job-seeking process is still largely seen as an individual enterprise. Most seekers take it on as a competition or as them against the world. Once they are hired, they view themselves as individual agents. Ordinarily, they focus on the task as theirs and try to carve out their territory. When this is compounded with the rational thought process, we get a perceived separation of the work self and the personal self. Therefore, "we have to work together, but we don't have to be friends." From this perspective, the other elements of dysfunction arise.

Chapter 2:
Relationship Building

I got a call from a small-town sheriff, asking if I could help with a problem with their 9-1-1 dispatch center. The concern was that they were experiencing repeated conflict within the dispatch team. He described the pattern that they were encountering. There would be a "blow-up" at some point, resulting in the need for a team meeting. During the meeting, some disagreements were worked out, and calm returned. However, the cycle that followed the meeting was that the calm was temporary. Gradually, the tension would return and build until the next "blow up." This pattern repeated for seven years. I agreed to take on the case, suggesting that I visit personally to see what was happening. My usual practice of conflict intervention was to schedule interviews with all the people in the organization. This usually resulted in two outcomes. First, the act of interviewing itself would calm almost everyone down. This is a simple matter of the Hawthorne effect. When people feel like they are being heard, they usually feel better. Second, it helps me to sort out the underlying issues.

In this case, it was clear to me going in that the meetings were not getting to the root causes of the friction. Rarely have I seen group meetings resolve conflict issues. The first problem is that there are far too many possible relationships in the room. Communication principles note that the number of relationships increases substantially as more people are added. If there are two people, there are three relationships: interpersonal, intrapersonal, and intergroup. Adding one person increases that to nine possible relationships. Adding another person increases that to twenty-seven. Since this case involved nineteen people, not including the managers, the number of relationships in the room is virtually impossible to manage. The resolution of the issues could only scratch the surface.

This brings us to the second problem in resolving conflicts with group meetings. Typically, there are individuals who will dominate the conversation. This may be a matter of extraversion vs introversion. It could also be a matter of more dominant personalities. Regardless of whatever is driving this dynamic, the result is that many issues are not uncovered. What I have seen is that the issues that are not addressed are the source of the building tension after the meeting. These are the main reasons I prefer individual interviews.

Remembering the two levels of each message points us to another dynamic in resolving conflict. The content message is rarely a source of long-term conflict. It is more likely the relational message that causes the problem. For example, if a person is to address another employee with the following message: "I need these files processed and stored by the end of the day." The content is pretty straightforward. However, the relational message may be another matter. The relational message is that they are in a position to make such a request. If they are the second person's supervisor, the relational message is congruent with the circumstances. However, if the first person is the one who reports to the second person, the relational message is incongruent and would likely cause problems. If the two are peers, there may or may not be a problem. If the two have agreed to help one another when one has a heavier load than the other, there is usually no problem. If they have not, there could easily be a problem.

During the interviews, I looked for a couple of things. First, I listen for relational messages. These are ordinarily implied and may be difficult to detect. As in the example, if one person instructs another to carry out a particular task, it is the relational message that causes the big conflicts. Then, I also listen for emotional messages. These usually indicate the intensity of the topic for everyone. They can also point to the primary conflict. Most organizational conflicts tend to center around a core dyadic conflict. It begins with friction between two individuals. Subsequently, each one will seek out allies. The goal for them is to justify how they feel. This might stem from a form of self-deception. I will get back to that later.

In this case, there were key messages that really stood out for me. Amazingly enough, every person during the interview would say something to the effect of, "We have to work together, but we don't have to be friends." That was a red flag for me. The fact that everyone said it and, with conviction, told me something very important about the team culture. It was clear that this was seen as a very important sentiment. I had come across this before, but this was quite stark. What was going on that resulted in this firm conviction? I suspected that this came from leadership, but could not pin down exactly how. I hypothesized that there were two probable sources. The first one would be what took place during the orientation phase of each person's employment. This is frequently where the tone of the culture is established. The other likely source was the perceived need to control one's emotions as a 9-1-1 dispatcher. That could be read as applying to their professional relationships as well.

There was another set of responses that pointed me in a different direction. Every one of the interviewees identified someone or a group that did not like them. At the same time, they all said there was no one they did not like. This is a rather significant disconnect. The first thing that came to mind was that only the second statement was likely to be true. The first statement was describing how other people felt, which one cannot know. The second was describing their own feelings. More to the point, this confirmed for me that there was practically no relationship-building happening in this group. The individuals were projecting their own feelings and insecurities onto the others. Unfortunately, it is rather common that people will arrive at negative conclusions about others if they are only guessing the intent of others. E. Terry Warner calls this a "psychologistic" process. (Warner, 2019) Briefly, he describes this as the way most navigate through life, essentially expecting that others intend to do them harm. Consequently, they are more likely to engage in offense-taking than not. The result of this practice is that they will respond to others as if the offense was intended and anticipated. This would result in the other person responding in kind.

Because the aggressiveness of the other is the 'uptake' achievement of the self-justifier, people in conflict with one another need not try to hurt one another to keep the conflict going indefinitely. They only need to worry about justifying themselves, for in this mode, each is able to turn almost any response of the other into an offense, and the other will be able to do the same reciprocally. (Warner, 2019)

Most of the time, this is a form of self-deception. If a person is inclined to believe others intend to offend them, no offense is required. They will contrive any action as potentially fitting the bill. This became very clear to me as I was conducting the interviews. I must admit that I had not completely understood what was going on at the time, but I knew that the ongoing conflict had taken on a life of its own. The most intriguing part of it was that the conflict arose from false premises. It became clear that no one entered the team with ill will against anyone.

I have worked with many groups over the years that exhibited similar behaviors and dynamics. One truly fascinating discovery was how often this was the case with people in human service occupations. These are people who care about the fate of other human beings. They were social workers, health care professionals, non-profit services, and counselors. One would think that they would be more likely to see the good in others. However, that is not what I found. Ironically, their conflicts were more intense than in other occupations. These were passionate people who elevated offense-taking to even higher degrees. I have spent many hours listening to tearful descriptions of how they had been mistreated.

The emotions are certainly genuine, but mostly based on misconceptions. This can only be explained by the self-deception that goes along with offense-taking. The deception takes on two forms: a belief in their own victimhood and one of the other's intent to harm them. Typically, through several hours of exploration and discussion, both parties discover that their perceptions were inaccurate. The second deception is the one involved with a person failing to honor their own integrity. For example, a person may recognize that a colleague is overwhelmed, but they don't offer to help. They will typically engage in a process of justifying this failure by attributing flaws to the other person or the need to defend themselves.

The huge question that presents itself here is how this can happen. One would think that reasonable people (and most of the people I interviewed are easily described as such) would not fall into such a state. It is primarily tied to the fact that people do not take seriously the need to embrace the work of relationship building. Most of us know that our relationships involve a lot of work. This is especially true of our most intimate ones. Somehow, the widespread belief is that work relationships do not require such effort. The predominant belief is apparently that the opposite is true. There is some thought that there are two selves: the personal self and the work self. Team members and managers alike remind me that personal lives should not interfere with their professional lives. I agree that personal issues should not contaminate our professional lives. However, there is an irony here. The practice of suppressing the emotions and stress of personal issues will adversely affect our work lives. Any time we suppress such things, it will cause us to lose focus and be constantly distracted. At the same time, I recognize that airing such challenges (especially if they become constant) is not helpful to the workplace. That is also the case in our personal lives as well. In all environments, we need to learn healthy ways of dealing with these challenges. I will expand on this later.

Frequently, in our communication processes, we try to conceal the two key elements to relationship building, i.e., the need for relationship and our personal emotions. This is largely a fool's errand. For example, how many times has someone started a performance conversation with, "Don't take this personally." Most of us know what the next word is, "but…" Perhaps we think this will neutralize the impact of the feedback, especially if it is particularly harsh. This is a *non sequitur*. What we are discounting here is that our work is very personal. Work is a primary form of human expression. We apply our creativity and invest our time in what we do. To infer that it is not personal is just doubling the negative impact. Besides, I don't know any other way to take things than personally. I am, after all, a person. I am sure it is one of those things we don't think through when we say them. We should remove that from our communication practices.

In effect, these two practices contribute to something very important. They de-personalize us in the workplace. This is a continued extension of the intention of the industrial organization. The idea from the beginning was to remove the person and only deal in positions. This is intended to accomplish a couple of things. The first is to make the positions more malleable. It is much easier to think in terms of dealing with inanimate objects than people. Managers can move them around, change them, and get rid of them and feel no remorse because it is "not personal." It also preserves the intent of a Rational society. A key element of Rationality is that it replicates a machine. It draws direct cause-and-effect relationships, and it utilizes interchangeable parts. It is little wonder that people believe they don't have to build relationships at work.

Much of the misunderstanding of workplace interactions is tied to the belief that the emotional, or affective, self should be irrelevant. Fortunately, recent developments in emotional intelligence are doing much to combat that mistake. (Goleman, Working with Emotional Intelligence, 1998) Goleman not only acknowledges that emotions are important but that we must work harder to appreciate their role if we want to be more successful. Emotionally intelligent people are more self-aware in terms of their own emotions and the impact they have on our work. They are also more "other aware" in terms of how emotions impact them, especially in regular interactions. The affective part of our psychology plays a larger role in how we work, especially in how we work with others.

Studies find that workers who are dispositionally higher in positive affect are *more* likely to leave their jobs if they are dissatisfied than are people who are characterized by low positive affect. (Judge, 1993) One reason behind this relationship is that for low positive affect individuals, the impetus to quit is small because they do not expect a new job to be more satisfying. (Gibson, 2007)

There are literally thousands of books and articles that argue that employees should be treated with respect and value. The general trend is away from what is called "transactional leadership." This is the long-standing practice of the boss being the decision-maker, monitoring the employee's work, and expecting compliance. Most credible authors and speakers advocate for a change to a more humanistic approach. I have observed many times that organizations take this seriously and try to make the changes. Far too often, these efforts are short-lived. The essential problem is that we are not attacking the root issue. In my earlier book, *Rational Gridlock*,[2] I presented a description of how so many organizations were tied to this rational thinking. (Edgar, 2011) This is one of the key consequences of such thinking. No matter how many times the reforms are tried, whenever a challenge arises, the organization will return to its rational roots. I will return to this later when I consider what actions we might take instead.

The key to relationship-building is interpersonal communication. It is clear to me that most people recognize this, especially those in

---

[2] This was published under my previous name, Patrick Edgar

leadership. The primary barrier is that people misunderstand what it is. Whenever I am asked to give a presentation or consult about communication, I get the same kind of expectations. The goal is to improve the way information is disseminated so that the messages are clear. On the surface, this might appear as a reasonable request. What I have discovered is that the tendency is to attack the wrong problem. There is generally more than enough information being shared in most organizations. However, there is much less understanding. Managers tell me that they are excellent communicators, and they make expectations very clear. That suggests that in their mind, the problem is with the receivers of their message. It fails to recognize that words do not have a universal meaning. Our use of language is anchored in images. As we learn to use language, we associate the words with images. Since we all have different experiences when encountering words, we have different images. This gets even more complicated when it comes to more abstract concepts. For example, we have different understandings of what it means for something to be "good" or "fair." These are not only associated with images, but they are also tied to values. So, when a manager tells an employee that they are doing a fair job, it will be interpreted differently. For some people, this is a positive remark; for others, not so much. Remember also that the message has two levels of content and relational. Without recognizing these filters, we tend to misunderstand messages far more often than we think.

Another issue in interpersonal communication is the considerable role played by the non-verbal and para-verbal aspects. According to some researchers, non-verbal communication may account for up to 90% of our communication. (Mehrabian and Ferris, 1967) The top figure is particular to certain communication events when conveying one's own feelings and attitudes. The general rule is that non-verbal communication accounts for around 60-70 % of our messaging. (Kudesia and Elfenbein, 2013) Nevertheless, that is quite significant and a largely overlooked part of our work behaviors. One aspect of this is the poor non-verbal communication behaviors when it comes to conflict. The most egregious is the use of email or the written word for dealing with conflict. The problem here is that the non-verbal is left out entirely, leaving it up to the recipient of the message to fill it in.

There are many common mistakes that I have seen when it comes to non-verbal communication. Eye contact is a vital element in successful communication. However, I have watched many people in organizations fail to consider this. For example, there is a tendency to continue looking at a monitor while someone is speaking to them. This not only interferes with any kind of relationship building, but it also reduces the likelihood that the message will be understood.

Interesting principles of communication I learned many years ago in my studies were based on Wiio's laws. They bear repeating here:

Communication usually fails—except by chance.

If communication can fail, it will.

If communication cannot fail, it nevertheless usually does fail.

If communication seems to succeed in the way intended, it must be in a way that was not intended.

If you are satisfied that your communication is bound to succeed, it is then bound to fail.

If a message can be understood in different ways, it will be understood in just that way that does the most harm.

There is always somebody who knows better than you what you meant by your message.

The more communication there is, the more difficult it is for communication to succeed. (Goldhaber, 1986).

In all the years that I have been observing organizational communication, I have found these "laws" to be largely true. I have found number 2 to be especially true. This is particularly the case when it comes to relational messages. The truth of the matter is that if we believe that "we don't have to be friends," then we are not likely to put in the work to improve our relational messages. One corrective of this is the widely recognized practice of using assertive language. Unfortunately, most people misunderstand the concept. When people speak of assertiveness, I usually hear them describing aggressive practices. The primary goal of using assertive language is to balance my needs with the needs of others. This requires one to be more self-aware as well as aware of others. It begins with our recognition of the difference between needs and wants. This is not always an easy exercise. We tend to confuse the two concepts regularly. Personally, over the years, I have discovered that my actual needs are far fewer than I thought. The complementary part of the process is to recognize the needs of others. The best way to accomplish this is to ask. That seems to be a rare occurrence in the workplace.

An equally important and related communication skill is listening. We spend more of our time with the opportunity to listen than we do to speak. It is an opportunity to listen because we are not very good at it. I have stated on many occasions that if I were allowed to teach one communication skill, it would be listening. For too many, the practice is to hear for an opportunity to respond. An active listener is one who is listening for meaning. The truth of the matter is that very few of us are taught how to listen. In our educational experiences, we are required to hear and regurgitate. To be an active listener, we need to ask clarifying questions and paraphrase what we hear to be sure that our understanding is accurate. This is another essential skill for relationship building. It is directly related to assertive skills. If we cannot listen for meaning and clarity of feelings, we cannot be aware of others.

Closely related to the challenges of listening and assertive language is a general resistance to self-disclosure. This does not mean that people at work should be revealing their deepest, darkest secrets. It means that people who work together should be able to admit when they are struggling with something. It is rather common for colleagues not to ask for help when they need it. This is probably an extension of rugged individualism. To ask for help is seen as a sign of weakness. The truth is that it is a sign of strength. When I can admit that I cannot do it all, it shows that I have the ability to recognize the truth. We cannot do it all and, more importantly, we cannot know it all. People are also unwilling to disclose their weaknesses at work. We all have strengths and weaknesses. However, we don't all have the same ones. The effectiveness of an organization lies in the diversity of its strengths. If we fail to acknowledge where each of us feels competent, then we will not apply this diversity effectively. The lack of self-disclosure is really an impediment to the effective use of abilities. We should not fear letting others know that we cannot do it all.

One of the primary obstacles to self-disclosure, and thus, relationship building, is the prevalence of gossip and complaining. These are two forms of false intimacy. The gossiper is a person who only talks about others. This throws up a barrier to anyone learning anything about them (except for a lack of trustworthiness). Gossip undermines the cohesiveness of the team. Not only does it sow resentment toward others on the team, but it becomes clear to everyone that they may be the next topic of conversation. The chronic complainer is closely related to the gossiper. The usual topic of conversation is tied to complaints about management or other team members. I have never left a "gripe session" feeling any better about my work life. If the only thing we can talk about is our mutual misery, it is unlikely that we will ever be able to focus on how we can make the situation better. These two forms of false intimacy are toxic to the work environment. They make relationship building nearly impossible.

Recently, at a workshop I was leading, I asserted the need for relationship building. I got a rather strong pushback on this. The participants stated that they didn't want to share personal information with their workmates. That prompted me to think this through a bit more. To clarify, the principle is to build relationships to facilitate the smooth operation of a team. We don't share our deepest secrets with every relationship we have. So, we would not do so at work either. Sometimes, such friendships may develop at work, but they are not necessary to accomplish the organizational mission. Instead, we need to be able to disclose our preferences and strengths. One effective way of doing this is to use some of the assessments that gauge these qualities. The two that I use are the Myers-Briggs Type Indicator (MBTI)® and the Kolbe Index®. When these are used to help the team, it is a fairly risk-free means of self-disclosure. I understand that there are some scholars who find these instruments to be pseudoscience. (Grant, Think Again, 2021) However, the purpose of using these is not for scholarly research. It is to encourage conversations about differing preferences and strengths. This is what I mean by relationship-building. While people don't need to hear about personal drama, it is helpful to recognize that sometimes they are distractions. In any event, what is disclosed is entirely a personal choice.

A related issue is the general resistance to diversity in the workplace. This is not about demographics as much as it is about differing personalities and strengths. It is widely believed that if people are generally alike, there will be greater efficiency and effectiveness. That does not seem to be the case at all. In fact, what happens is that the groups will either fall into groupthinks or cliques.

Groupthink is a phenomenon that occurs when a group of well-intentioned people makes irrational or non-optimal decisions spurred by the urge to conform or the belief that dissent is impossible. The problematic or premature consensus that is characteristic of groupthink may be fueled by a particular agenda— or it may be due to group members valuing harmony and coherence above critical thought. (Psychology Today staff, n.d.)

Groupthink is a phenomenon wherein the group is so homogenized that creativity is extremely limited. The solutions to problems will follow the same general pattern. Any novel ideas or creative practices are extremely unlikely to occur. In fact, novel ideas are more likely to be suppressed if they occur at all.

The other alternative is cliques. This happens when seemingly like-minded people form blocs within the organization. Ordinarily, such blocs are defined by their opposition to some other group or individual. A great deal of time and energy is wasted within the organization to sustain these cliques. They increase gossip and complaining and fuel additional conflict. These are probably the most egregious blockades to relationship building. There tend to be tacit rules associated with maintaining cliques. The most important one is that everyone is expected to choose a side. One is either with the clique or against it. There can be no neutrality. Once a person is in the clique, it is extremely difficult to get out. There are rarely direct confrontations between the cliques. Rather, the norm is to engage in passive-aggressive behaviors. Communication breaks down completely. Consequently, creativity and competent problem-solving are severely impaired. I have been absolutely amazed at the prevalence of these dynamics in organizations I have either worked in or consulted. In fact, I have referred to it as middle school behavior. It is nearly impossible to distinguish between these adult behaviors and those of middle school children.

The lack of relationship building directly contributes to the other aspects of dysfunction. It is the primary indicator of serious issues in how we organize. Since people have excused themselves from building relationships with their coworkers, an enormous amount of time is wasted through unhealthy conflict, poor communication, inappropriate distribution of responsibilities, etc. I am convinced this happens because we are stuck in the Industrial model, coupled with our commitment to individualism. As we unpack the other factors of dysfunction, I believe it will become clear how this plays out in the workplace and our other organizations.

Chapter 3: Arrogance

The primary source of arrogance, according to the National Institute of Health (NIH), is the resistance to accepting the limits of our own knowledge. Cowen et al suggest that there are three types of arrogance: individual, comparative, and antagonistic. They identify six progressive components: distorted information and limitations in abilities, overestimation of one's information and abilities, resistance to new information about one's limits, failure to consider the perspectives of others, belief or assumption of superiority, and denigration of others. (Cowen, et al, 2019)

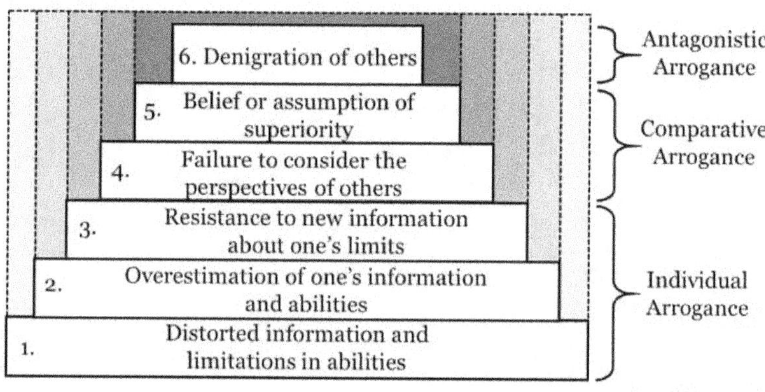

(Nelson Cowan, 2019)

An excellent example of this was an instance in a seminary for second-career vocations. One of my classmates, who was an M.D. and had a Master of Public Health degree, pointed out that the food served to the seminarians was entirely inappropriate for older men. I brought this to the attention of the vice rector. He utterly rejected the idea and said the food was fine. What would prompt a person whose only credentials were in theology to argue against the medical doctor? I think you know the answer. Part of the key to understanding arrogance is the unwillingness to acknowledge that one's abilities are limited. Herbert Simon broadly refers to it as "bounded rationality" (Simon, Administrative Behavior: A Study of Decision-Making (second edition), 1957). Simon proposed: "to replace the global rationality of economic man with a kind of rational behavior that is compatible with the access to information and the computational capacities that are actually possessed by organisms, including man, in the kinds of environments in which such organisms exist." (Simon, Administrative Behavior: A Study of Decision-Making (second edition), 1957) The crux of his proposal was directed at economics and decision-making. The tendency in the field was to use quantitative models for decision-making, implying that these models yielded factual data that enabled rational decisions. The problem, according to Simon, was that there are always limitations to the data that is available to address the issue at hand.

Adam Grant, in his book *Think Again*, suggests that such a limitation can lead to a particular kind of arrogance, known as the Dunning-Krueger effect. "It's when we lack competence that we're most likely to be brimming with overconfidence." (Grant, Think Again, 2021)

I can tell you from my own experience that this is widespread, especially in management. In most of my consultations, the manager would present themselves as quite competent in their style. They told me they were quite clear in laying out expectations and were quite enlightened when it came to dealing with their employees. It didn't take very long to discover that this was not true. In the interviews of individual team members, they would describe behaviors on the part of the manager that were anything but enlightened. I would hear stories of obvious favoritism and conflict avoidance. Often, the stories were rather alarming. Managers would fail to acknowledge successes or, worse, take credit for the accomplishments of other individuals on the team. Generally, the more a manager elevated his/her skills as a leader, the more likely it was that the opposite was true. Even in my most recent consultation, I found a leader who suggested that he was very creative and open-minded in his leadership style. With a little exploration of actual behaviors, it became clear that his behaviors were more along the lines of "command and control." It is very difficult to tell these managers the truth. In this case, when I did so, he fired me as a consultant. When it comes to consulting, it appears that telling the truth is not a great business model.

This tendency matters because it compromises self-awareness, and it trips us up across all kinds of settings. Look what happened when economists evaluated the operations of management practices of thousands of companies across a wide range of industries and countries and compared their assessment with managers' self-ratings… Overconfidence existed in every culture, and it was most rampant where management was the poorest. (Grant, Think Again, 2021).

This has been borne out by my own experiences as a consultant and member of the organizations.

This should not be confused with certain pathologies, however. Sometimes, this overestimation of abilities or knowledge can be confused with sociopaths or narcissists. This is more likely a defense of the manager's ego than anything else. There is some evidence that this exhibition of confidence is concealing something quite the opposite – the Imposter Syndrome.

Impostor syndrome (also known as impostor phenomenon, fraud syndrome, perceived fraudulence, or impostor experience) describes high-achieving individuals who, despite their objective successes, fail to internalize their accomplishments and have persistent self-doubt and fear of being exposed as a fraud or impostor.[1] People with impostor syndrome struggle with accurately attributing their performance to their actual competence (i.e., they attribute successes to external factors such as luck or receiving help from others and attribute setbacks as evidence of their professional inadequacy).[2] Psychologists Clance and Imes first described impostor phenomenon in 1978,[2] and it came to widespread public attention after Clance's 1985 book.[3] Clance originally identified the syndrome among high-achieving professional women, but more recent research has documented these feelings of inadequacy among men and women, in many professional settings, and among multiple ethnic and racial groups.[4], [5] (Bravata DM, 2020)

The authors go on to say that Imposter Syndrome is not a recognized psychiatric disorder. (Bravata, 2020) Ironically, this is frequently concealed by an overt bravado. According to Silverman et al,

Although arrogance is conceptually related to personality characteristics like narcissism, hubris, and confidence, there are important distinctions that set arrogance apart from these other traits. Narcissism (or self-love) involves fantasies of self-grandeur and excessive self-admiration that can occur in the absence of others. Arrogance on the other hand, is manifested in interpersonal contexts by disparaging others. (Stanley B. Silverman, 2012)

This is not to say that there are no cases of managers as narcissists or sociopaths. There may very well be a number of them. That is not my concern here. My focus is on the garden-variety arrogant manager or other team members.

Distorted information and limitations in abilities. This is undoubtedly the most common form of arrogance. Most, if not all, have experienced this. Parents see it firsthand in their teenage children. This includes all kinds of sensory and perceptual illusions, memory mistakes, attention deficits (we all have a certain degree of ADHD), mistaken facts, simplifications, assumptions, slips of the tongue, and reflexes. (Nelson Cowan, 2019) These, on their own, are problematic but not particularly harmful if they are addressed. We all have times when our perception of something is inaccurate. It is common knowledge that eyewitness accounts of events can be inaccurate. However, this may be a bit overstated. Recent studies have shown that the closer to the event that witnesses are interviewed, the more accurate they are. However, they can be easily influenced by peers, interviewers, or events. (John T. Wixted, 2018) A healthy response occurs when we acknowledge that we don't have perfect information and that our memory may not be precise. The road to arrogance is set when we are convinced that our perceptions and recollections are facts. I have seen this in my own family when stories are shared, and the versions are rather different from one another.

Many of the interpersonal conflicts I have intervened in are matters of different perceptions. In one instance, the two people involved described very different scenarios of the same incident. In fact, they were so different that it took me a while to recognize that they were talking about the same occasion. To help them resolve their conflict, we had to work together to reconstruct the incident, so the versions were much closer. Often, the issue behind a conflict arises from the distortion associated with offense-taking. Because the receiver of the information took offense, the memory of what was actually said is inaccurate. It may be a matter of different inflection or interpretation of a word or phrase. I remember an incident where I responded to a person, "Of course, you do." What I was saying arose from the work we had done on personality and conation. She commented that she thought the phrasing in some of the questions in the assessment should be changed. I was pointing out that this is a normal reaction. She took it to mean that I was criticizing her as being arrogant. I took a few minutes after the class to discuss this with her, and the matter was resolved. These kinds of misunderstandings may be brief flare-ups if dealt with immediately. They can also evolve into long-term conflict if not clarified.

Overestimation of one's information and abilities. This second phase is rather crucial. It is one thing to have limitations in knowledge or ability. It is quite another to fail to recognize it. The best example is the Dunning-Krueger effect. This phenomenon is quite common in organizations. Sometimes, it can be a matter of inflating one's abilities in interviews. I imagine that many people would say this is necessary. After all, the interviewee is competing for a position. This is a very unfortunate aspect of how we treat interviews. Job interviews should not be a competition for a prize. The purpose should be to achieve the best fit. As such, it should be a matter of both the interviewer and the candidate establishing whether or not this will be a good match for each. This harkens back to the lack of relationship-building. From the very beginning, this is pushed to the back of the process. Unfortunately, it comes down to the person who can project the most confidence. Sometimes, skilled interviewers can pick up on overconfidence. The problem is that there are very few skilled interviewers.

This becomes even more significant when choosing a manager/supervisor. As stated before, far too many managers admire their own leadership abilities more than is warranted. For me, when I meet with managers to begin the consultation, excessive confidence is a "red flag." This is an indicator that I won't be able to help the organization very much. If I don't say everything the manager wants to hear, I will likely be dismissed, either conceptually or literally. I am not even talking about the higher levels of arrogance here. Those managers probably would not be seeking help to begin with.

One of the best examples of this phenomenon is the case of a human services/education organization. The manager presented himself as quite enlightened. He knew the right things to say and showed that he was interested in improving the dynamics of his organization. However, it became clear that this wasn't necessarily being put into action. The members of the team were frequently sniping at each other and tended to be very critical of their colleagues. This was something of a surprise to me. One-on-one, they all seemed like nice people. I wasn't sure what was going on to cause this. On further exploration, I discovered that this kind of behavior had been going on for quite some time (years). There had been earlier attempts to help the group. In some of the efforts, some progress occurred. Unfortunately, the outcome was backsliding shortly after. It became clear that the organizational culture was deeply embedded as one of conflict and isolation. One instance demonstrated this. Apparently, two individuals who worked in the same unit had not spoken to each other for years. I found this rather curious.

Why was this being tolerated? My conclusion was that leadership was not addressing conflict. If such a blatant occurrence of conflict was not being treated, then I could only assume that the more subtle forms were not as well. The probability of long-term correction of the dysfunction was rather low given such a circumstance. The message being sent by the leadership was that unhealthy conflict was tolerated. It did not sound like enlightened management to me at all.

Resistance to new information about one's limits. This is very common in dysfunctional organizations. I have witnessed this on more occasions than I can count. Most of us have experienced this firsthand. One place that stands out for me is in the classroom, of all places. I am not speaking of the university classroom so much. Although it did happen. This occurred more in the professional development classes for in-service managers and workers. For example, most of the time, when I was teaching about motivation, I would explain that money is not a motivator. This would very frequently yield immediate pushback. Although I presented well-documented evidence to support this, people would argue that it could not be true. What they didn't understand was the difference between motivation and hygiene factors. Hygiene factors are those that will not increase satisfaction, but the absence of them can increase dissatisfaction. These are things like money, benefits, and awards. Motivators are things like intrinsic rewards, such as the feeling of a job well done. Motivators are internal, and hygiene is largely external.

How many times have you heard someone say "but we've always done it this way" as a response to change? This common response to proposed change or any questioning of why certain procedures exist is really saying, "I really don't know why we do it this way." Although this may not sound like it, it is a form of arrogance. Essentially, the message is that the best way to do something has already been achieved, and we don't need to try anything else. As long as people resist change, it suggests that they have already arrived. Whenever I encounter someone who infers that they have already arrived, so to speak, I see big problems. This is a clear message that they are not interested in any new ideas.

There is a twist when it comes to resistance to change, however. Frequently, what is understood to be resistance may not be resistance at all. This can be more a matter of ambivalence than resistance. It is likely a disconnect between a person's knowledge, preferences, or strengths. Kathy Kolbe asserts that there are three parts of the mind: cognitive, affective, and conative. (Kolbe, Pure Instinct: The M.O. of High Performance People and Teams, 1993) The cognitive is the part about learning and experiences. All learning occurs through experience. Our education is an experience. This part of our mind is always changing because we are always experiencing it. The affective includes our motivation, values, and emotions. This is formed fairly early in life and changes a little over time. The conative relates to our natural strengths. Kolbe describes it as an instinct, and it never changes. It is how we naturally strive to solve problems. (Kolbe, Pure Instinct: The M.O. of High Performance People and Teams, 1993)

When changes are proposed to processes or policies, there is a strong probability that they may not connect with one or more parts of the mind. This causes a certain amount of stress. If it is cognitive stress, the respondent either doesn't understand the change or it doesn't fit with their current knowledge. If they refuse to learn more about the change, then arrogance is definitely in play. If it is affective stress, it either goes against their values or preferences. This is a matter of arrogance if the person refuses to examine their values. If it is a matter of personality, it could be arrogant if it is more about believing that one's preferences should outweigh everyone else's. If it is a strain on conative strengths, it is unlikely to be a form of arrogance. However, there are ways to address this without being obstructive. I will address this later. In any event, the important consideration is whether or not resisting new information is at the center of the motivation to resist.

Failure to consider the perspectives of others. During one of my earliest consultations, I interviewed the director of the county roads department. As we discussed the issues that involved poor morale in the department, I sensed a disconnect. I had already interviewed all the members of the team. So, this was my debrief of the findings. He kept talking about all the good things he had done over the years. It was like I hadn't said anything at all. I became curious about what was happening. I asked him directly if he had done all these things and why there were still morale issues. He replied that it was because the people in the department didn't appreciate him. This made no sense to me. So, I followed up with, "If you have done what you say, why don't they appreciate you?" He answered that they just didn't understand what he was doing. I then showed him the results of the interviews, noting that they did, in fact, mention what he had done, but these were not the issues. The more I pressed him to see that he needed to address the issues that they had raised, the more he repeated his claim that they didn't understand. They were just ungrateful. Needless to say, this was a very frustrating conversation. It was clear that he was not interested in what the employees had to say. I realized that this consultation was going nowhere. I submitted my report to the county commissioners. I included my recommendations, but the director was probably going to resist any of them. Since the County Surveyor, who was also the director of the roads department, was an elected position, there was little they could do. The only solution ultimately was to change the county charter and change the position to an appointed one.

This stands out as one of the more obvious forms of arrogance. Even in the face of compelling evidence that the employees were not happy with how the department was managed, he was convinced that he was doing a great job. As I have continued to be a consultant over the years, I have discovered that this is rather widespread. It may be a matter that the management positions are going to people's heads or that they become so isolated from the day-to-day activities that they essentially live in a bubble. The other part of this, ironically, is tied to the people around them. People expect managers to be highly skilled and smarter than everyone else. I had a case that demonstrated this perfectly. The team members in a unit I was consulting with complained that the manager didn't know how to do all of their jobs. I explained that it isn't necessary for a supervisor to know everyone's job. Rather, the supervisor needs to know how to coordinate the jobs and provide the resources for everyone to be successful. A sure way to increase arrogance is to tell leaders how wonderful they are.

This is not just a matter of managers in organizations. This kind of arrogance can be found at all levels. I had an instance of consulting with a state agency that was experiencing significant conflict issues. Through the process, I discovered that much of the conflict centered on one individual. It was clear that she was very unhappy. On one occasion, my colleagues and I gathered the whole team in a classroom to provide training on dealing with conflict. The mood of the room was rather upbeat, with lots of conversation happening. As soon as the troubled individual walked into the room, the entire atmosphere changed. Everyone suddenly became quiet, and eye contact went down. It was downright chilling. I interviewed her a few days later. She described her 17 years with the agency as being constantly battling over the same issues and struggling with her supervisor. I asked her, "Have you had the same supervisor all this time?"

"No," she responded, "I have had five different supervisors." I then asked her if she could see the common denominator. To her credit, after a moment, with a bit of a wry smile, she said, "That would be me, wouldn't it?" We then talked about how she really felt about her job. It became clear that she was miserable. More to the point, she just did not work well with other people. She openly resisted other ideas and felt that she was being disrespected. Fortunately, for her and the rest of the team, she recognized that she needed to find a different job, one that would grant her much more independence. This isn't always the best solution to this problem of arrogance, but it is frequently. I simply reminded her that life is too short to be miserable in your job.

Belief or assumption of superiority. These higher forms of arrogance are the most destructive. This is especially the case for anyone in a management role. Such people do not take feedback well. They tend to speak over others and raise their voices when asserting their point of view. It is destructive to the organization because it limits creativity and flexibility. Silverman et al describe the impact of such arrogance on organizations quite well:

In sum, arrogance can be thought of as a cluster of behaviors that communicate one's superiority and importance relative to others (Johnson et al, 2010; Leary, Bednarski, Hammon & Duncan, 1997). These behaviors include disrespecting colleagues and their ideas, purporting to be more knowledgeable than others, avoiding blame and/or pinning blame on others, and discounting feedback... It is noteworthy that arrogant behavior is typically not associated with actual superior performance or knowledge. (Stanley B. Silverman, 2012)

While teaching professional development classes for state agencies, my colleagues and I would encounter this regularly. Many times, when there were managers and supervisors in the same room, they would dominate the conversation. They spent so much time praising themselves as enlightened leaders that they missed the expression of frustration from those who reported to them. Over time, I learned to recognize the potential for arrogance when interviewing managers or supervisors. This became a "red flag" for a poor leader. Whenever they described how they had done such a great job, and they couldn't understand why there were problems with their team, I suspected that they were the problem. The challenge here was to get this point across to the manager. These tended to be my least successful interventions. The client would say the right things in terms of the changes they needed to make, but rarely carried them out fully. Over time, I learned that the better strategy was to ask more questions. Using something of a Socratic method, we both were able to discover some better strategies.

Denigration of Others. This, of course, is the most destructive layer of arrogance. It creates a toxic environment in which it is common for people to criticize others and avoid accountability. A couple of examples illustrate this more clearly. I was hired by the state to conduct an analysis of the Aid to Families with Dependent Children (AFDC) program. In the collection of the data, it became clear to me that the administrators of the program had a rather negative opinion of their clients. One of the ways that I gathered data was to simply sit in a public assistance office and listen. I was amazed at some of the discussions among the employees. They clearly labeled their clients as lazy or dishonest. The data I had collected from the clients showed them to be quite the opposite. The vast majority (82.3%) of the clients did not want to be on assistance. They were trying to hold things together as well as they could. They faced challenges of needing help with childcare, transportation, and skills development. The stereotype of multi-generational dependence was not shown to be true in the data. The average amount of time on assistance was less than 18 months. Unfortunately, since the service providers had such a negative view of the clients, the experience of relying on assistance was unpleasant, but it was also unproductive. When asked, the providers were unable to tell me what happened to the clients who left the programs. When I asked the advocates in the non-profit groups, they told rather dismal tales of people who were homeless and worse. Part of the reason this happened is that they were treated so poorly by the staff. Arrogance is necessarily an action toward others and is easily detected by the target. (Graeme Mitchell, 2024)

Arrogance is highly destructive in an organization, especially if it is exhibited by the leader(s). It interferes with creativity and suppresses initiative in others. It also increases the incidence of intention to leave the organization. The cost can be substantial due to a lack of high performance and high turnover. (Graeme Mitchell, 2024) I consider my own journey a case in point. I was working at a university as an assistant professor. I thought it was my ideal job. I love teaching and engaging with some of my colleagues. However, many of the other members of the department were quite arrogant. They denigrated their colleagues and put down my efforts at innovation. The classroom experience was terrific. The other parts of the job were dreadful. It got bad enough that I resigned from my tenure-track position. This was not an easy decision, but the work environment was just so unbearable that I dreaded going to work each day. Many times, the comments and criticisms were so offensive that I could not believe what I was hearing. In terms of a career decision, it was probably seen as foolish. On the other hand, in terms of my wellbeing it was necessary.

Arrogance is also a huge impediment to relationship building. No one is going to open up in an environment where they are being spoken over and ignored. If the rest of the team members are aware that they and/or others are being denigrated, there is no way that they will risk expressing their opinions or discussing their needs. It does not matter if the arrogance is on the part of leadership or other team members. The tendency will be for almost everyone to keep their heads down and remain isolated. Consequently, the best possible creativity and problem-solving will not happen. Add these things to the higher attrition rates, and the organization is going to be quite dysfunctional.

Chapter 4:
Lack of Trust

Trust can be a difficult thing to define. Generally, it is a sense that another person will do me no harm. Brené Brown probably gives the best description in her "anatomy of trust." (Brown, 2017) Her use of the acronym, BRAVING, is an excellent way to break down the elements of trust:

Boundaries—You respect my boundaries, and when you're not clear about what's okay and no okay, you ask. You're willing to say no.

Reliability—You do what you say you'll do. This means staying aware of your competencies and limitations, so you don't overpromise and are able to deliver on commitments and balance competing priorities.

Accountability—You own your mistakes, apologize, and make amends.

Vault—You don't share information or experiences that are not yours to share. I need to know that my confidences are kept, and that you're not sharing with me any information about other people that should be confidential.

Integrity—You choose courage over comfort. You choose what is right over what is fun, fast or easy. Any you choose to practice your values rather than simply professing them.

Nonjudgment—I can ask for what I need, and you can ask for what you need. We can talk about how we feel without judgment.

Generosity—You extend the most generous interpretation possible to the intentions, words, and actions of others. (Brown, 2017)

I can certainly add nothing to that. Building trust is a major factor in relationship building. Unfortunately, it happens rarely in the workplace. This is partly because we have excused ourselves from doing this in organizations. It goes back to the belief that we don't have to since work is not personal. I recently realized the significance of the term "work-life balance." We use it regularly. When I think about it, I realize that it implies that work is not a part of life.

Lack of trust is also caused by some very unfortunate human tendencies. One is self-deception and the other is *ressentiment*. These two interact to cause us to be more wary of our colleagues than to be cooperative. This is not something that we give much thought to. Rather, it more likely occurs because we don't really reflect on it. One could say it is our default mode. Unless we reflect on it and catch ourselves doing it, it happens rather on its own.

Terry Warner spends a great deal of time considering self-deception in his book, *Self Betrayal.* (C.. Terry Warner, 2019) The source of the self-betrayal is what he calls "psychologistic." (C.. Terry Warner, 2019) This is essentially a mindset wherein the individual believes it is necessary to be prepared to defend oneself from others. Consequently, the interactions between colleagues can be viewed as rather treacherous. When this is the case, it takes very little for conflict to arise and trust to be eroded. This is not a matter so extreme as paranoia, but it can become that. It is more of a tendency to be cautious in relating to others in the workplace. I have seen this in many, if not most, of my consultations. I discovered it during the interviews. The respondent describes an event or series of events that, from the outside, seem rather trivial, even harmless. However, the emotions run high, frequently involving tears. This aroused my curiosity in my earliest experiences in consulting. It wasn't until I came across Warner's work that I began to understand. If a person is thinking psychologically, they are likely to take offense at seemingly harmless comments or behaviors. The alternative would be to clarify what a person intended in what they said or did. It is amazing how rare that is. The result is more than a simple misunderstanding; it can result in an ongoing battle.

Both concepts come into play here—self-deception and self-betrayal. They are related ideas but not the same. Self-deception is a complex process that is very common in human beings. For example,

A survey of university professors found that 94% thought they were better at their jobs than their average colleague" (Gilovish 1991, p. 77). Are university professors exceptionally adept at self-deception? Perhaps not. "A survey of one million high school seniors found that ...*all* students thought they were above average" in their "ability to get along with others... and 25% thought they were in the top 1% (ibid.) (Mele, 2001)

The challenge is trying to arrive at some clear understanding of what is happening. The first consideration is whether it is intentional. Can a person really fool themselves into believing something if they are at least partially aware that it's not true? There seems to be little agreement on this in philosophy and psychology. On the intentionalism side, the argument is the belief that this is a strategy to protect the ego. This is accomplished by either not giving any attention to contrary evidence or by a form of confirmation bias. Anna Galeotti argues that self-deception is a complex mixture of things that we do and that happen to us; the outcome is, however, unintended by the subject, though it fulfills his [sic] practical, though short-term goals. She suggests more of an" invisible hand" approach, suggesting that it's a collection of manipulations of evidence that results in the deception. (Galeotti, 2012) Some argue that it is a matter of what a person pays attention to that allows self-deception. The person chooses what evidence matters in terms of what they believe. We can see that in what people choose to read or view. (Lynch, 2013) Confirmation bias is when we only accept any evidence that supports what we already believe to be true. The question remains whether this is intentional. On the non-intentional side, the idea is that people may simply allow their thoughts to govern what they believe, and really don't reflect on what they are doing. They tend not to reflect on how they come to conclusions on what to believe. It is probably a little of both. What is more important is how aware they are of their choices. Far more people lack a sense of self-awareness than one might imagine. When I have taught classes that involve self-awareness, most people are surprised at what they learn.

There are others who suggest that deception is not exactly something one does intentionally. For example, David L. Smith suggests that it may be more of a matter of getting to a successful endpoint.

The most that can be said is that if self-deception exists and is distinct from wishful and fretful thinking in virtue of its success-aptness, then the teleofunctional theory provides an account of it that is more satisfactory than those provided by either of its better-known alternatives. [standard non-intentional or intentional] (Smith D. L., 2014)

The point here is that self-deception may be used as a means of getting to a better situation or position. One might deceive themselves to protect their ego or to overcome some obstacles."

Self-betrayal is a different form of self-deception. This is tied to our likelihood of not complying with our own moral code. Arbinger provides an excellent description of this process. For example, if I notice that one of my colleagues is overwhelmed with work. At the same time, I have plenty of free time because input is low. The moral sense that I would/should have offered to help my colleague. However, I do not make that offer. The thought process that follows is to view my colleague and me in different ways. I might think that my colleague is not very efficient or that there have been plenty of times when they weren't doing anything. I might see them as incompetent or just plain lazy. I see myself as a victim in this instance. Helping my co-worker only enables her to be incompetent, or it means I have to take on an additional burden. These are all forms of justification. (Arbinger Institute, 2018) This justification will directly influence the relationship between the coworkers. Keep in mind, the other person has not done anything to warrant mistreatment. Unfortunately, the justifier will treat them as if they have. This will necessarily undermine any possibility of trust.

If the self-deception and self-betrayal continue, it will likely impact not only the relationship between the two of us but will also have a long-term impact. If I believe the things that are a result, that others intend to offend me, and that the other person has character flaws, I will likely treat that person accordingly. I might be short with them or ignore them. When they experience my behaviors, they will likely react in kind. They may avoid me or even belittle me as not much of a "team player." This will initiate a repeated cycle. As long as we see each other in these terms, we will continue to behave accordingly. Arbinger refers to this as a collusion. (Arbinger Institute, 2018) Since we are both likely to be looking for justification, the common way to do that is to seek allies.

I might make comments like, "I don't know what she actually does, do you?" This is a clear indicator, implying that I don't think she works hard or is responsible. If the other person agrees with me, then they are my ally. If they disagree with me, then I will assume they are her ally. Consequently, the team becomes divided and forms groups of alliances. The ability to develop trust is completely undermined at this point.

One of the underlying factors of self-deception is its influence on how we see others. Arbinger describes how human beings tend to turn other people into objects. (Arbinger Institute, 2018) This is drawn at least partially from Martin Buber's *I and Thou*. (Buber, 1970) According to Buber, we truly enter into the human experience with our recognition of the other. This means that we acknowledge them as people with feelings, hopes, dreams, and challenges. They are not exactly like us, and it is in this recognition that we come to know ourselves. This is similar to Hegel's concept of self-consciousness. He claims that the only way we come to know ourselves is through the consciousness of others. (Hudson, 2010) The key point here is the reality that when we see people as objects, then we can excuse ourselves from building trust or relationships. At first glance, it can be hard to believe that we do this. I can cite times when we are in traffic or encounter someone on the sidewalk with a cardboard sign. Those are common points where we are likely to see them as objects. We may see them as irrelevant or obstacles. The larger concern, to me, is when we see others as an instrument or vehicle for our own purposes. People can sense when this is happening and react accordingly.

I have seen these dynamics in so many organizations—those that I have worked in and those I have consulted. I must admit that I did not understand what was happening at first. I assumed that this is just the way it is. I think we draw that kind of conclusion all too often. In my earlier experiences, the kind of advice I offered was generally okay but didn't really get to the heart of the matter. I thought it was just a matter of people behaving badly, and they needed a reminder about being kind to one another. After a while, it became apparent to me that there was more to it. This is what prompted my research into how long-term conflicts happen in organizations. More to the point, what was sustaining them for so long. On the surface, it just made no sense. People had to recognize that what they were doing was irrational. The difficulty the conflicts created for the organization and the people in it was terrible. On top of that, it was clear they did not know what to do about it, especially the supervisors. Then I came across the material from Buber and Arbinger. This began the process of clearing it up for me.

I had a case in a county government that demonstrated these dynamics quite well. I was called by the county administrator to help with a problem he was having with the staff. He described how the employees were constantly at odds with one another. There were instances where people actually bumped one another in the hallway. They tried to get people to talk it through and resolve their differences. It just didn't work. I asked what other kinds of things they tried. They told me they would move desks around or put them in other rooms to separate people who were fighting. I was astonished. My goodness, it's not the third grade! I agreed to take the case and set up the interviews. I must say there were a lot of intense emotions in the interviews. People were angry, frustrated, stressed, and frequently came to tears. It took a lot of digging but I finally discovered a source. I won't describe it as the source because there were others.

It began with a squabble between the human resources director and the payroll manager. During one of the payroll cycles, there was an error that affected several employees. It turned out that the HR office had not passed on critical information regarding how a particular deduction was to be applied. I inquired as to why they didn't pass on the information. The HR manager told me that she should not have to do so because the payroll manager should have already known about it. The payroll manager, on the other hand, was not aware of the change because she wasn't at the meeting where it was decided. The payroll manager then complained to the county administrator that HR was trying to undermine her job. The HR manager then complained that the payroll manager was setting her up by not making the change in the deductions. Subsequently, each of them had been talking to others about how the other one was not doing their job. It wasn't long before the two alliances had formed. It even got to the point where there was a very public fight between people from the two sides at a youth basketball game in town. Of course, this whole thing could have been avoided if the two individuals had met regularly to discuss any changes that might affect either or both of them.

To complicate matters, the two alliances sided with opposite candidates in a county election. On that point, I advised the county administrator that such direct involvement in a political campaign by public employees was against the law. That being the case, he should have put the word out that they were not allowed to do so. While that would not have stopped the conflict, it would have removed at least one layer of it.

This was clearly a case of offense taking and self-betrayal. The offense occurred when the HR manager informed the payroll manager that the mistake had been made and she needed to correct it. One would think this to be a straightforward adjustment, and the problem would be resolved. However, the payroll manager took offense that she was being set up. If she weren't in psychological mode, she likely would not have interpreted it that way. The self-betrayal occurred when the HR manager failed to pass on the information. One would think that it would be entirely reasonable to make sure the payroll office had the information. In the interview, it was quite clear that she had gone through the process of justification and came to view the payroll manager as an object ("She should have known. Why should I cover for her mistake?"). Bear in mind that the payroll incident was the beginning of the process. After that, the collusion just built up, and the two groups engaged in multiple events of offense-taking and self-betrayal.

Self-deception (including offense-taking) and self-betrayal are generally individual phenomena. There is also a social phenomenon that is at play here, and it definitely undermines trust. In the 19th Century, Friedrich Nietzsche suggested that a sentiment developed in the Western world that drove much of the political and social behaviors. He called is "ressentiment." (The Polemics of Ressentement, 2018) This concept has been largely ignored by academics and leadership authors. However, this may be a mistake.

The general idea is that society is divided between the nobles and the slaves. These terms, of course, are rather dated. So, I will take some liberty here and identify the division as between the oligarchs, the middle class, and the working class. The dynamics still apply. The oligarchs exhibit resentment toward the other two groups. They believe that they are an uncontrollable rabble that lacks the character to function well in society. They generally don't act on this resentment because they can't afford to isolate themselves from it. The middle class, in the meantime, resents both the oligarchs and the working class. They resent the oligarchs for being greedy and arrogant. This is coupled with envy for the lifestyles they flaunt. They resent the working class for draining resources and exhibiting boorish behavior. The working class resents both the oligarchs and the middle class. They see the oligarchs as controlling the system and a lifestyle that is excessive. The middle class they see as arrogant and hypocritical.

Some have claimed that we have moved past ressentiment since we have moved into the post-industrial society. (The Polemics of Ressentiment, 2018) However, others argue:

Except that a pervasive sense of cynicism, the rise of populism, fundamentalism, anti-intellectualism, and the whole culture of naming, blaming, shaming, and claiming by people who experience themselves as victims despite living in affluent societies, challenges us to reconsider the problem. (The Polemics of Ressentement, 2018)

Ressentiment is more than the English equivalent, resentment. It includes a bit of envy and intolerance.

The more we compare ourselves with others, the greater the ressentiment we will experience over any perceived inequality. Ressentiment here is understood as the sour-grapes syndrome: since we cannot get what we want, the grapes must be revalued as undesirable. We thus seek compensation in the unconscious affirmation of our inferior position, as we continue to rely on the conviction as to the superiority of ruling-class expressions or values, which we equally transgress and repudiate. (The Polemics of Ressentement, 2018)

Most of the discussion surrounding ressentiment is centered on the political-social levels, wherein people are both envious and frustrated that they believe they have no alternative. (Balcomb, 2021) We see the elements of it in various movements like MeToo and Black Lives Matter. We also see it in groups that may or may not experience inequality. Much has been written about the resentment experienced by white males (primarily young white males). Their perception is that they are being left out and blamed for all kinds of antisocial behaviors. Interestingly, there need not be any necessity for any perceived injustice to be factual. (Merrick, 2020) Fukuyama contends that there is more to ressentiment than just envy or revenge. He adds the notion of dignity to the mix. (Balcomb, 2021) This can explain the force behind the identity politics that we experience today.

…it is often accompanied by what Nietzsche called the "falsification of the tablets of value," which also means that it may lead to alternative mental constructions of reality that might result in delusional perspectives that can have dire social and moral consequences. (Balcomb, 2021)

Each group is reeling from the assault, or perceived assault on their dignity. The appeal of "make America great again" reflects this sentiment quite well. There is a perception of lost power or distinction. Thus, there are two sides contributing to the current profound division. There are those who feel that they have lost their position of privilege, namely white males. Then there are those who feel that they have suffered humiliation and depravation for too long, blacks, women, LGBTQ, etc.

This ressentiment permeates society and becomes the lens through which everything is viewed. It also influences how we perceive and interact with organizations. In case after case, I heard managers and employees complaining about each other. It seems that complaining about management is a favorite pastime in organizations. What is interesting is the complaints usually de-personalize their target. It is very common to encounter conversations about management that habitually use that term. Rarely have I listened to such complaints directed at managers by name. At the same time, most of my interviews with managers involved generic criticisms of employees. Many times, it was as if they were talking about altogether different organizations. A key feature of ressentiment is the labeling of others, along with scapegoating.

All of this resentment carries over to the workplace. People in the workplace feel that they have suffered humiliation by management and corporate leaders. Social inequalities carry over to the workplace as well. Ressentiment is deeply ingrained and not always obvious. I have witnessed it many times in my interventions. Sometimes, it will be quite overt, and people will state it right up front. More often, though, it is subtle, and employees and management alike will focus on other issues as the cause of their friction.

It is interesting that people in the workplace want to believe that we have reached a post-racial period, along with other forms of intolerance. That is clearly not the case at all. I base this on some very straightforward observations. When I was working at a university in the south, I noticed that people were polarized whenever they had the chance. They would tend to gather with others who looked like them or thought like them. This is a phenomenon known as *homophily*. (Miller McPherson, 2001) The neighborhoods were clearly separated. The most segregated day of the week was Sunday. The white and black populations went to their own churches. Even in the Catholic community, there was separation, with the Latinos going to separate liturgies that were in Spanish. If people separate themselves in their so-called personal lives, there is very little chance that they will engage in any relationship building in the workplace.

In my interviews with people in organizations, I found frequent labeling of others. The separation doesn't just stop with the failure to build relationships. It also tends to result in stereotyping or labeling. The most common stereotyping I have found is with generations. The older workers would complain about the younger ones and vice versa. The problem with stereotyping is that it undermines trust. For one thing, it creates a cycle that reinforces itself. For example, the older workers and managers would complain about the Millennials and the Gen Z workers having no work ethic. Unfortunately, that usually resulted in the young people being treated like they had no work ethic. This would take on behaviors like constantly correcting them or micromanaging. After a while, what happens is that the young people have no work ethic. They just wait to be told what to do and avoid taking any initiative. The dynamic worked in the opposite direction, as well. The young people would believe that the older workers were averse to using new technology. So, they would avoid requiring them to make the change or have them trained in the new technology. Consequently, the older people did not seek out new technologies. The use of stereotyping is a powerful force to undermine trust.

An issue closely related to both ressentiment and stereotyping is scapegoating. This can be directed at people both in and out of the organization. Inside the organization, it is very common for employees and managers to establish who is to blame when something goes wrong. It could be directed at someone in the same unit or another unit. If it wasn't anyone within the organization, it was about the customers or the citizens. The conversations that I would overhear in the public assistance offices come to mind. Things were not going well, so it must be that the clients were misbehaving. The complaints by the county HR and payroll person were another perfect example of looking for someone to blame. Scapegoating takes on a social dimension as well. The most recent election has demonstrated this quite well. The problems in the nation are pinned on the immigrants or the educated elites, or both. Blaming or scapegoating undermines accountability. If we are looking for someone to blame, then we don't have to look at ourselves.

Ressentiment has clearly developed in our organizations. The titles may be different, but the attitudes and behaviors are not. The equivalent of the nobility is the upper management, as distinct from middle management. The slaves are the rank-and-file workers. Upper management resents the working people for not performing to their standards or for being just plain lazy. This is particularly directed at younger employees. I have already mentioned the unfortunate stereotypes that are directed at young workers. Managers I have interviewed frequently mentioned the lack of a work ethic. They also criticized young workers for not showing much respect. Consequently, the tendency is to treat the young people accordingly. What they fail to recognize is that the young employees do have a work ethic and believe in respect. The truth is that their concepts of each other are different from those of the older folks. Their work ethic is tied to purpose. They do not see any point in engaging in work activities that do not contribute to the purpose of the organization.

This makes sense. As technology natives (i.e., they have always had it as part of their lives), they have witnessed digital technology performing repetitive, mindless tasks. It makes no sense to them to do things that computers or robots can do. Their concept of respect is also a bit different. While older people may believe that one should show respect for bosses (or elders), they don't see it that way. They believe that respect is mutual. So, it is easy to see how the level of resentment can be widespread. The important thing here is that ressentiment is very common. Such a state only undermines trust.

An unfortunate trend in the current economy is the growth of the "gig economy." This is a practice of hiring contractors instead of permanent employees. The increasing number of contract employees broadens the number of people in a precarious position. (Calalini, 2019) As contractors, they are at greater risk of unemployment. They are also responsible for their own retirement and health care plans. An equally disturbing trend is the hiring of larger numbers of part-time employees. This includes job-sharing employees. Developing alternative job designs can be highly problematic. It creates a circumstance where relationship-building is virtually non-existent. The large number of remote workers makes building trust extremely difficult. I will discuss how this may be dealt with later. The more significant consequence is the impact on building trust. It is nearly impossible to make any progress toward a trust-laden organization if people are largely just passing through.

The bottom line, so to speak, is that most organizations have difficulty building trusting relationships between leadership and the rank-and-file and between employees. This contributes to all kinds of dysfunction. If a significant number of people in an organization are processing the world around them psychologically, which leads to various forms of self-deception, including offense-taking, it will be nearly impossible to find greater efficiency. It will also lead to wasted energy caused by miscommunication and distortions. I have personally witnessed this in action in many organizations. Sometimes, it is so rampant that I have concluded that the people have not progressed past middle school social behaviors. If we throw ressentiment into the mix, we have a real problem that leads to rampant suspicion and outright sabotage. As a scholar of public administration, I consider this a major source of our discontent with government. Agencies need to be nimble and responsive. If they are caught up in these dynamics, they can be neither.

Chapter 5:
Lack of Transparency

Ordinarily, when we speak of transparency in organizations, we mean from leadership to the rank and file. It is equally important at all levels. It is true that transparency between the executives and the rest of the organization is important. This can lead to more consistency in the understanding of the mission and practices throughout the organization. It is also true that the failure to be transparent can result in a lack of trust and undermine employee engagement. However, the lack of transparency within the ranks can be just as destructive. A couple of cases help illustrate this.

My colleagues and I were asked to provide a workshop for an agency that was undergoing some major changes. To pull this off, we needed to divide the group into three classes. This was due to the lack of space more than anything else. The group essentially self-divided into the middle managers, the upper managers, and the new and front-line workers.

During our conversation with the first group, the middle managers, they expressed frustration because they felt they could not get any answers from upper managers. The upper managers, on the other hand, were not aware of the middle managers' quandary. Their explanation for not providing answers was that they didn't have the answers.

My immediate response was, "Why not just tell them that?"

The third group was not aware that there were any issues with the changes and assumed all was well. It is interesting that each group was unaware of the perspective of the other two. The lack of transparency was clearly a reality all around. Our intervention was essentially one of being a conduit for the information that should have been shared from the start. If the various players were more open about their concerns or general perspective, most of the difficulty implementing the change would have been averted.

The second case was one I consulted with a local government. I received a call for assistance from the local city council. About a year earlier, the council had managed to get approval for a grant to install a sewer system, replacing the septic tanks that were then in use. They were very excited about this, but soon trouble ensued. Several members of the community were upset that this decision was made without consulting them. Their issue was that they would have to pay to get hooded up with the new system.

Consequently, they produced a petition to put the new system on a ballot initiative. Having gotten enough signatures, the initiative proceeded, and the citizens voted down the sewer system. The city council found itself in quite a pickle. They were forced to return the grant money to the state agency. This never goes over very well. They were unsure what they could do next. After some discussion, we decided to conduct a community needs assessment. The method I chose was more of a census than a survey. This required that we deliver questionnaires to every household in the community. After we tabulated the results, we reported them at three community meetings to ensure the highest turnout. We learned a great deal about the town, but the most important thing was that it appeared that the citizens seemed to recognize the need for the sewer system. Subsequently, we convened a community meeting to develop a strategic plan. When all was said and done, the top priority set by the citizens was the sewer system. Had the city council gone to the public initially, a whole lot of trouble could have been avoided. As a postscript, we also assisted the town in securing a new grant and a program that assisted with the individual household hookups.

In each of these cases, and almost every other case I have worked on over the years, the problem is transparency. This is not necessarily always a matter of the leadership failing to be open about decisions or situations to the rest of the organization. It is equally important that people throughout the organization be more open about concerns and practices. For many reasons, the protection of information is viewed as a way to preserve stability and job safety. From my experience, the opposite is generally true. By concealing information, reactions and decisions are made based upon false premises. It also adds to the suspicions of coworkers and between management and labor. Complete transparency is not always necessary or desirable. Certainly, anything that involves what should be confidential information about an individual should not be disclosed. There are also interpersonal dialogues at different levels of the organization that do not need to be shared. However, generally, this is overdone. Many times, it goes back to the fear that uncertainty or needing help is seen as a weakness. This is worth examining more fully.

Much of the issue lies in our commitment to hierarchy. On many occasions, the response to my suggestions regarding relationship and fluid leadership is "but we have to have hierarchy." To understand this concern, it may be useful to examine what role hierarchies play in organizing. In the hierarchical model, a key feature is the control of information. The intention is that all information should move vertically in the organization and not horizontally. This allows the managers to control information. If any data needs to be relayed to another branch of the hierarchy, then it must proceed up the channels until it reaches the first level that the branches have in common. This supports the illusion of control over information.

Part of the issue is what level of information is being controlled and/or shared. The closer information comes to knowledge, the more it is controlled at the top. There is an important distinction between data, information, knowledge, and wisdom (Bernstein, 2009). The collection of data moves up the hierarchy to become information. This is a more useful form for decision-making. As the information is accumulated and analyzed, it becomes knowledge. In many cases, it is this knowledge that is reserved for the managers, as they have the overall responsibility for how it is to be used. Over time, this knowledge becomes wisdom. This is the territory of those who should have a longer-range vision for the organization. This wisdom is important for the success of the organization. Hierarchy certainly has its place. There is evidence to support the idea that using hierarchy appropriately can lead to better decision-making. (Jurgen Mihm, 2010) In cases where complex problems are being addressed and multiple sections are involved, hierarchy facilitates the process by collecting the information from the sections and making quicker decisions. This would not work as well if the organization were too decentralized. (Jurgen Mihm, 2010) However, hierarchy is not always effective or necessary. The important point is to know when hierarchy is necessary and when it can be an impediment.

Sometimes, relying on hierarchy is the very thing that prevents transparency and can be more of a problem than the solution. A personal experience demonstrates this. Several years ago, I was serving in the Navy Reserve. During a drill weekend, the commanding officer came into the room where I was working. He went to the executive officer and explained what he wanted done with a particular document. The executive officer, in turn, went to the chief petty officer and explained the same thing. The chief petty officer went to my immediate supervisor and explained the same thing. At this point, my supervisor came to me with the same document.

I immediately said to him, "You're not!"

"What do you mean?" he responded.

"You're not going to explain to me the same thing I have already heard three times!"

"It's the chain of command."

I retorted. "No, that's just stupid!"

Turning to the commanding officer, I said, "With all due respect, sir, I have a wonderful command of the English language. Wouldn't it make more sense to tell me directly what you wanted? If we weren't in the same room, it is very likely I would have gotten it wrong."

He responded with the same chain of command argument. I should point out here that I already had my Master of Public Administration degree, which explains my reaction. Needless to say, I didn't drill again since I had already met my obligation. The point is that hierarchy got in the way of both efficiency and transparency in this case.

Closely related to the fascination with hierarchy is the desire for command and control. This is a type of transactional leadership. The transaction is that managers lay out expectations, which typically include things like standard operating procedures. Workers are to carry out those expectations in exchange for rewards. Managers will also closely monitor the workers and provide rewards or sanctions depending on how well the tasks are carried out. These organizations also tend to be heavily rule-bound. In order to maintain this order, information is usually confined to the top managers. The expectation is that everyone in the organization will comply, keeping things consistent. In many cases, the top levels of the organization maintain what Frederick Herzberg called "mystery systems. (Herzberg, Mystery Systems Shape Loyalties, 1984) He uses the metaphor of a black box to describe how information and processes are carried out beyond the view of the rest of the organization. How decisions were made and sometimes, even who was involved, are kept from the workers. In such a system, transparency is intentionally withheld. Generally, the lack of transparency further erodes trust. (Moore, 2023)

There are instances where transparency is not advised. This mostly has to do with the reliability of the information. If leadership has information that may be a result of rumors or inference, it is wise to withhold it until it is verified. This certainly works in the context of the workers. Moore suggests that three questions be addressed before sharing information. "1. Is it True? 2. Is it kind? 3. Is it useful?" (Moore, 2023) I can certainly agree with that suggestion. When considering transparency, we must balance the need for sharing information and the potential that such sharing may cause. It is more likely that the lack of transparency stimulates the increase of unreliable information. The vacuum created by failure to share information is filled with rumor and innuendo.

One particular area where transparency plays a huge role is when there is a significant change experienced by the organization. Change frequently causes discomfort on teams. It doesn't seem to matter what the change is or who it affects. Much of the literature about change presents the response to change as resistance. The belief is that people don't like change and will naturally resist it. That is simply not true. People experience change throughout their lives. I understand that sometimes it feels like one loses control over their lives.

However, they also repeatedly overcome the sense of lack of control and make the needed adjustments. Jason Clarke, who cleverly notes that if people don't like change, someone should notify the fashion or tourism industry. (Clarke, 2010) While the comment may be a bit snarky, there is truth to it. People seek out change regularly. Something else is going on in the organization: ambivalence. This comes about because people have a hard time connecting with change in one or more parts of the mind. Kathy Kolbe identifies the three parts of the mind: the cognitive, the affective, and the conative. (Kolbe, Pure Instinct: The M. O. of High Performance People and Teams, 2004) The cognitive is that part of the mind that is created by our experiences. Everything we experience adds to our knowledge. By the way, this includes education. Education is actually an experience. We tend to apply a false dichotomy by separating the two.

The affective includes our emotions, preferences, and values. This part of us changes a little over our lifetime. For example, many psychologists suggest that our personality is likely formed by the time we are four years old. There will be some slight changes to it; absent any trauma, it will remain the same. There are significant changes as one develops and matures and encounters different experiences, but the basic traits tend to remain the same. What is important is how we identify personality. The two major models of personality that I have encountered are Myers-Briggs Type Indicator® (MBTI) and what is known as the Big Five. MBTI measures four dimensions of personality, resulting in 16 different personality types. (Myers, Introduction to Myers-Briggs Type (Seventh Edition), 2015) These are fairly broad generalizations that are useful in understanding some responses to situations. These traits are the ones that tend to be stable. The Big Five, on the other hand, uses different categories. These include extraversion, agreeableness, conscientiousness, openness, and neuroticism or emotional stability. (Christopher J. Soto, 2020) The Big Five are also considered far less stable and change with maturity. Personally, there is truth in both. The basic tendencies noted in MBTI do stay with us through our lifetime. However, the more volatile ones in the Big Five also influence our behavior. In either case, personality does not determine behavior. It influences it, sometimes strongly.

The third part of the mind is the conative. This relates to the natural instincts that we have as humans. It is particularly notable as it relates to problem-solving or striving. We should not understand this as an instinct as seen in other species. Other species act on instinct without any knowledge of either their existence or purpose. We, on the other hand, can go against our instinct because we still possess free will. In the form that Kolbe describes, we have four general action modes: fact finder, follow through, quick start, and implementor. (Kolbe, Pure Instinct: The M. O. of High Performance People and Teams, 2004) We fall somewhere on a continuum in each of the action modes. The important feature of this framework is that it is important to focus on working within our strengths. To do otherwise will cause stress.

"…the conative dimension of an attitude reflects on individuals' evaluations of an attitude object that are based on past behaviors and future intentions to act..In the context considered here, because an employee facing a newly proposed organizational change is responding to a novel event, the conative dimension is more likely to reflect intentions than past behaviors." (Pidarit, 2000)

The relationship between these psychological concepts and transparency is extremely important, especially when it comes to dealing with change. Rather than viewing the response to change as one of resistance, it is more likely one of either ambivalence or disconnection. If the change does not connect with one or more parts of the mind, the individual experiencing the change will appear to respond negatively. This could take the form of apparent uncooperative behavior. This is more likely them trying unsuccessfully to connect to the change. Figure 1 shows the likely response to change. Clearly, there are more ways that change can be ineffective since there are more ways for the disconnect to occur than not. How does this relate to transparency, then? Leadership should strive to involve the entire team as much as possible when going through changes. Typically, either leadership or some task forces are the ones who develop the plan for change. Then it is presented to the rest of the organization. It must involve the entire time, much earlier than that. I go so far as to recommend that it should occur during the process of defining the problem being addressed. That way, the widest amount of information may be used in understanding what needs to be addressed.

Figure 1: Does the Proposed Change Fit?

Cognitive	Affective	Conative	Description
Y	Y	Y	Total Commitment.
N	N	N	Total opposition.
Y	N	N	Understand, can't commit, and stressed.
Y	Y	N	Understand, can commit, but stressed.
N	Y	N	Don't understand, can commit, but stressed.
N	Y	Y	Don't understand, can commit, and a little stressed.
N	N	Y	Don't understand, can't commit, and a little stressed.
Y	N	Y	Understand, can't commit, and a little stressed.

The importance of involvement with the statement of the problem cannot be overemphasized. When I supervised thesis projects or dissertations, I found this to be the most crucial stage. I pushed the candidate to make sure that they had defined the problem correctly so that they could avoid much bigger problems when actually conducting the research. If the research design is done correctly, the project usually just falls into place. The same is true when considering change in an organization. If there is enough time put into the development of the problem, the solution is more likely to succeed. The frontline workers are likely to add insights related to detailed elements of the problem, as well as anticipate any problems that may arise when making the change. This is definitely an area where transparency is crucial.

…what some pay perceive as disrespectful or unfounded opposition might also be motivated by individuals' ethical principles or by their desire to protect the organization's best interests. It is worth entertaining efforts to take those good intentions more seriously by downplaying the invalidating aspect of labeling responses to change as resistance. (Pidarit, 2000)

Two particular "mystery systems" in most large organizations are budgeting and officious language. Most of my experience has been in the public sector, but I have had some experience in corporations. Public budgeting systems are particularly complex. Over the years, Congress and state legislatures have added more and more accountability devices. This leads to so many rules that it's nearly impossible to navigate the steps needed to operate. It's actually quite ironic that efforts to increase accountability result in convoluted systems that make it appear that governments are wasteful. The real problem is that the frontline government workers arc usually confused when it comes to their own budget.

In my most recent experience as a bureau chief in state government, I was mostly confused. My bureau was proprietary, meaning that it did not get general funds but had to make enough money through fees for services to operate. We then paid the agency where we were housed for the rental of office and classroom space. We also paid for our equipment and supplies. The rules required that we have a balanced budget. This meant not only could we not be in a deficit, but we were not allowed to have more than 60 days' worth of funds on the books. On several occasions, I was advised that I had hit my spending limit.

I responded by asking, "Do I have money in the account?"

"Yes, you have plenty of funds in the account, but you have hit the limit in your budget."

"So can you increase the limit?"

"That has to be approved by the governor's office."

After some haggling, we were able to get the approval. The most confusing part about it was that when I would get the financial statement at the end of each quarter, I couldn't make head nor tail of it. The same document said that I had a deficit and a surplus. Sometimes, it would say that revenue was well ahead of projections, but that we were projected to have a deficit at the end of the year. Even after ten years of working with this system, I had no idea how it worked. The transparency problem was that I didn't know where the budget figures came from. Consequently, I didn't know what we could or could not do financially. In the end, we had an enormous surplus that we could not spend.

Budgets and their procedures are usually managed by the financial professionals. They tend to use their own language and mysterious calculations. We kept our own records in my bureau. So, we know what our revenues and expenses were. However, the numbers didn't look anything like the ones on the report that I got from the financial people. After a couple of years of this, I just ignored the reports and relied on our internal data. The challenge is that sometimes, management would caution me that I was spending too much money. In many ways, this undermined any trust that I had in managers. Since I couldn't verify their numbers, I was in no position to defend my bureau. This is not the only time in my 55 year career that the budget calculations made no sense. The best way to describe this is disempowering.

The use of complex language is another obstacle to transparency. One of the services my bureau provided was to train people in plain language. We used the documents coming from the agencies that we assisted as examples of convoluted language. On one occasion, my team and I were reviewing documents for an agency. We were not off to a good start. The first sentence in the document had 89 words! Even worse, the three of us could not figure out what it said. We all have advanced degrees and could not understand it. This was a document that went out to members of the general public. If the professionals who worked in state government could not understand it, what do you suppose was happening with the people who got the document? After some discussion with the people in the agency, we were able to figure out what was intended. We rewrote the opening of the document. That sentence was changed to two sentences with 10 and 9 words, respectively. This is not just a problem in government agencies. I have had many occasions where I received a document from insurance companies or health care facilities, where I had no idea what they were saying. The significance of using this kind of language in our writing is that it also disempowers the receiver. Overly complex budgets and the use of officious language are both barriers to transparency.

…the direct relationship between transparency and OC [organizational commitment] was shown to be stronger than that of the mediating variables. These findings serve to highlight the emerging importance of transparency for stakeholders within the organization. It comes as a surprise that transparency was shown to be more predictive of OC than supervisory support. (Salazar, 2017)

Chapter 6:
Untrained managers

There is a long-standing tradition in modern organizations that is generally ineffective and, often, highly destructive. People are promoted to supervisory roles based exclusively on seniority. They have either been very effective in their jobs or have achieved a close relationship with management. This assumes that supervision or leadership are natural skills. This results in supervisors or managers with low skills. Leadership is not inherent in human beings. It involves some rather sophisticated skills. Frequently, the result is either a micro-manager or a "hands-off" manager. Neither of which is actually management. To top this off, there are few opportunities for professional development in terms of leadership skills. What is typically made available are quick-fix, one-size-fits-all workshops that have little staying power.

In the ten years that I directed a professional development center for my state, it became abundantly clear that this is a serious area of neglect. My staff and I observed literally hundreds of people coming through our classes who really had no business being in a leadership role. For example, one of our classes was in conflict management. Part of the class required the participants to complete the Thomas-Kilmann Instrument® (TKI), which measures conflict styles. The number one style for these people in leadership training was "avoid." (Killmann, 2023) It wasn't even close. The very last style used was "collaborate." This would indicate that these supervisors were likely unable to deal with conflict on their team. When asked about this, the normal response was that they did not know what to do. Unfortunately, what tends to happen is that conflicts only fester. Often, conflict spreads beyond the initial people and divides teams. If managers were skilled, most of this would be avoided.

We also found that the people given supervisory responsibilities believed that their job was about command and control. Few see their responsibility to care for their team members. This is one of the more significant issues with untrained managers. This is primarily because they are not trained prior to assuming the role. The management style they adopt is the one they were typically subjected to themselves. What it comes down to are two things: improper selection criteria and poor interviewing skills for the selection committee. The selection criteria focus on the candidate's knowledge, skills, and abilities (KSAs) and length of service. Of course, requiring the necessary KSAs is important, but this doesn't address the skills needed to be a supervisor. These should be discovered before interviewing any candidates. The interview should be focused on goodness of fit. Selection committees should be looking for evidence that the candidate has the necessary "soft skills" (a term I reject because these may be the hardest skills of all). In many cases, the length of service could be a problem. There is a good chance that the candidate learned how to supervise under a manager who practiced the old command and control method, sometimes referred to as transactional leadership. Personally, I would prefer a candidate who acknowledges they have a lot to learn about leadership skills. That shows they are open to learning and respect that it is an entirely different skill than the ones they have used in the past. Herminia Ibarra also suggests this, reminding new leaders that "what got you here, won't get you there." (Ibarra, 2014)

Even if a supervisor is selected based on evidence of the right skills, it is important to recognize that these skills need to be regularly updated. Leadership is an ongoing learning process. If I am promoting someone from one supervisory level to another, it is imperative that I review carefully their track record as a leader. An obvious piece of evidence would be the success of their team. A great deal has changed in the field of leadership in the past couple of decades. So, it is essential that supervisors get regular updating of skills. I don't see a lot of that in the field. Instead, more organizations are relying on pre-packaged training programs. These are usually very appealing but don't have a lot of substance. Quality training needs to be delivered in a setting where supervisors can engage with the facilitator, especially with the opportunity to ask questions. When relying on online classes or large conferences, there is little to no opportunity for this. In my experience as a professional development trainer, the dialogue resulting from questions was usually the most valuable and effective part of the classes. Many times, the content of the class does not apply to the circumstances of the participants. Unfortunately, many of the presentations and workshops I have attended amount to more performance than education. I have heard hundreds of complaints about training, literally, claiming that it was useless. This can be corrected through appropriate professional development programs. I will discuss later how this can be done.

The biggest problem with the lack of leadership training that has any substance or impact is the tendency for supervisors to either be passive ("hands-off") or micromanagers. It appears from the research that the passive style is far more destructive than one might expect.

…followers who perceived their leaders as passive-abusive showed significantly worse outcomes on physical health and perceived organizational support than followers who experienced the passive pattern. This was not the case with psychological health. When psychological well-being was defined broadly (GHQ-12: Goldberg & Williams, 1988), to include both affective and cognitive indicators (e.g., one's ability to concentrate, make decisions, cope with stress and feelings of worthlessness and depression), we observed no difference between the passive and the passive-abusive patterns (i.e., supervisors who are perceived to be avoidant and disengaged are as detrimental for followers as supervisors who are perceived as both passive and abusive). However, when psychological well-being was defined more narrowly as emotionality (e.g., feeling cheerful, in good spirits, calm, relaxed, interested; Bech, 2012), we see hints that the lower affect was associated with the passive pattern. (Study 2) Thus, behaviors associated with the passive pattern (e.g., distant, avoidant) are particularly sensitive to affective forms of psychological well-being. (Amanda J. Hancock, 2023)

The choice of a more passive style is frequently associated with a lack of knowledge of leadership skills. Many of the newer managers that I have interviewed expressed feelings of being overwhelmed and not sure of what they could do. It is no wonder they would be avoidant and distant. From the employee side, it can be frustrating for a number of reasons. In many of my consultations, employees would describe their concerns about the passive manager. One issue that comes up frequently is when one of the team members is misbehaving in some way. Their colleagues complain that it is unfair to the rest of the team when they habitually show up late, take extended breaks, leave early, or neglect their job altogether. When the passive supervisor fails to take action, the rest of the team questions standards and the idea of fairness. They tell me that they report misbehavior, but nothing happens. Over time, others begin to behave in a similar way. The ones who uphold their professionalism begin to resent what they see as a double standard. Teamwork is lost, and performance declines. It is also incredibly difficult to rein this in if it has been tolerated for some time. Furthermore, it creates a huge challenge for the next person to take the supervisor role.

The other extreme of micromanagement is equally problematic. This is not unusual when the person who becomes the supervisor is very skilled at their duties as the worker. They tend to assume that others should perform the same way.

Commanding other people to behave in a way that aligns with your interests while denying theirs cannot create strong teams, precisely because it goes against the way human brains work. ... At work, command energy can be destructive in peer relationships and between supervisors and direct reports. People, naturally wired for autonomy, resent feeling "bossed around." I tell clients that command energy is like gravity; it's ubiquitous. Leaders hardly notice that they're using it, but it profoundly affects everything they do. (DiGangi, 2023)

The micromanager makes more work for themselves than is necessary. When they decide how everything is to be done, the team members will tend to stop taking any initiative. These managers may have the best intentions, but they cause more harm than good. Such detailed supervision is harmful to morale and can result in a lack of motivation in employees and even high turnover. Instead of being actual guidance or mentoring, it becomes an impediment to team development. These behaviors tend to discourage other team members. This is particularly harmful to younger employees. Ryan and Cross found that Millennials are particularly resistant to this kind of leadership. (Cross, 2024)

Julia Milner describes a rather different version of micromanagement – the motivational micromanager. (Milner, 2024) They really do have the best intentions. They want to motivate their teams and infuse the workers with energy. The nicest and most supportive managers can still be know-it-alls. They want to be coaches for their team, but their enthusiasm overrides their restraint.

Motivational micromanagers will approach an employee with a smile on their face and a warm greeting. They make it clear that they are "here to help." There's a lot of head nodding and comments like "That sounds great," "Excellent idea," and "I like how you're thinking." But at some point, during the conversation, the manager will inevitably sprinkle in advice and tidbits of wisdom. They will say "Why don't you try this?" or "Don't you think you could do it that way?" or "Have you ever thought about using the following approach?" or even more direct, "First go and do this, then that". (Milner, 2024)

This is directly related to a lack of training in leadership practices. It is worth pointing out that this becomes an ongoing problem. Such leaders may actually move up in the organization even though they are ineffective as leaders. One of the most common comments we heard in our leadership classes was "My boss should be here." A major part of the problem is that such leaders are unaware that they are not effective. This is tied to what is called the "Dunning-Krueger effect." Simply put, this is when incompetent leaders are unaware that they are incompetent. They are actually brimming with confidence in their leadership skills. (Dunning, 1999) I have personally witnessed this phenomenon in my consulting work. Many times, when I begin the conversation, the manager will tell me how they are doing all the right things. They will describe their style as empowering or caring. However, as I interview other members of the team, it becomes clear that the managers are not particularly self-aware. What is described to me is typically one of the two extremes of either passive or micromanaging. These have been my most challenging consulting experiences. I am dedicated to telling the truth in my consulting work. So, I will be honest with these managers and explain how they are part of the problem. It turns out that this is a lousy business model for consulting work. I do it anyway.

The extremes of passive or micromanagement are not the only behaviors that must be called asshole behaviors of managers. The research literature describes a whole range of behaviors that are equally so. Individually, they may not be as common, but collectively, they are very common. Wallace Burns describes a broad range of misbehavior on the part of supervisors. (Burns, 2017) He identifies three main categories of poor behavior: abusive, bullying, and toxic.

According to Tepper (2000) and Tepper, Duffy, and Ensley (2004), abusive leaders are characterized by their "injurious actions that include public ridicule, angry tantrums, inconsiderate actions (i.e., rudeness, favoritism, non-contingent punishment, and coercion...Ashforth (1994) argued that tyrannical leaders are "distrusting, condescending and patronizing, impersonal, arrogant and boastful, and rigid and inflexible. They take credit for the efforts of others, blame subordinates for mistakes, discourage informal interaction among subordinates, and deter initiative and dissent. (p. 374) (Burns, 2017)

Of course, this doesn't cover the whole range of abusive behavior, but it gives us a pretty good idea of what it means. Bullying bosses are those who identify targets (either individuals or groups). They direct harassing, offending, or exclusionary behaviors at their targets repeatedly. The difference between the abusive and bullying boss is the targeting itself. (Burns, 2017) The continuous nature of bullying has an extensive impact on the target and the organization. The level of stress created by bullying leads to high levels of anxiety at both the state level (directly a result of the stress) and the trait level (a part of the person's personality) (Mengyun, 2020). This leads to poor performance and negative organizational citizenship behavior. In other words, it is bad for productivity. Leaders are considered toxic when they inflict harm on their fellow team members, employees, and other stakeholders. They use harsh tactics that are notably malicious. They may employ strategies like a lack of concern for the well-being of employees, a lack of integrity that shows them to be cynical, corrupt, or untrustworthy, and an insatiable ambition. (Burns, 2017) These destructive behaviors are not only harmful to the members of the organization. They also consume a ton of energy that could go to improved productivity or quality.

The list of behaviors provided by Pelletier is particularly revealing:

Publicly ridiculing an employee's work.

Hanging a "wall of shame" board to post employee blunders.

Lying to employees to get his or her way.

Blaming others for the leaders' mistakes.

Taking credit for an employee's work

Asking an employee to falsify productivity figures to meet a goal.

Mocking employees as a display of humor.

Throwing a tantrum when goals are not met.

Promising you a promotion if you do something that involves bending a company policy.

Demoting an employee without giving a good reason for the decision.

Failing to respond to the concerns of employees.

Telling employees to work, not think.

Lying about the organization's performance.

Telling an employee that he or she is not a team player.

Creating contests between two employees where winning involves downplaying the work of others.

Ignoring employees' comments.

Greeting all of your coworkers but ignoring you.

Threatening to terminate a coworker, even if the statement is made in a joking manner.

Making false statements about competitors.

Yelling when a deadline is missed.

Making an employee feel as though his or her job is in jeopardy.

Raising a voice when his/her point does not appear to be accepted by employees.

Asking one of your coworkers, "Is this the best you can do?"

Threatening to deny an employee's vacation request if a deadline is missed.

Saying to an employee, "You just don't understand the problem."

Coercing employees to accept his or her ideas.

Bending the rules to meet productivity goals.

Inviting specific employees to social events and excluding others.

Acknowledging others' contributions to a project but not yours.

Failing to disclose the reasons behind organizational decisions.

Slamming a fist on the table to emphasize a point.

Making employees work until the job is done, even if it means they must work all night.

Not sticking to the plan of action.

Encouraging good performers to put pressure on poor performers.

Giving resources to the departments whose functions make the leader look good.

Continuing to do things the old way.

Reprimanding employees when they make mistakes.

Inviting a select few to an important meeting.

(Pelletier, 2010)

This is a pretty good list of asshole behavior provided by real-life respondents. One really has to ask how it is that a supervisor can treat people like that. The answer has two parts. First, it is how they were treated by their supervisor. This is the model they had for supervision. Second, they don't see them as people. As Martin

Buber described it, they do not enter into an "I-Thou" relationship but an "I-It" one. (Aguas, 2024)

In both my consulting work and my professional development classes, I hear many common reasons for not using more effective leadership practices. The most common is the belief that they are not allowed to do these things and that they are powerless. Their perception isn't that they won't change their practices; it is that they can't. I reject this sentiment completely. First of all, no one is powerless. We all make choices in our work. It may not be practical to change everything we do overnight, but it is possible to start with the simple things. There is no reason a supervisor can't change their use of language so that the other team members are empowered. For example, one can easily change from "do this" to "how can we make this better?" Milner provides another list of excuses for failing to move to more empowering and coaching methods. I find these to be incredibly accurate. They also demonstrate how a lack of training comes into play.

As a leader, I need to be an expert and provide all the answers. This is not just something believed by the supervisor but by many members of the team. This is a classic mistake. This only invites micromanaging and does not improve team performance. The supervisor is responsible for enabling a team to perform at its best. That means that they strive to remove impediments and encourage creativity. The challenge in the workplace today is to enable the team to be problem-solvers. That means that everyone has skills and natural creativity. Applying only the knowledge and skills of the supervisor fails to draw upon a most crucial resource.

Empowering others is listening, showing empathy, and asking questions – I don't need training for that. This is most common as we move up the chain. Upper-level managers are convinced that they have all the skills needed to get better. As one who provided such professional development services, this is the most frustrating barricade of all. The person who decides that they have made it and they are a superior leader is in trouble. In leadership, we deal with enormous diversity. There is always more to learn. The sad truth is that if one does not invest in continuous leadership training, the cost in time and resources will only increase. One of my mottos in my organization was "we can all always get better." These empowering leadership skills do not come naturally.

I don't have time to empower others. To put it bluntly, you don't have time not to empower others. If you are the one who believes that you have to provide the answers to problems, then you will be micromanaging, and the team will not develop the skills needed to solve problems. Once again, this wastes the most valuable resource on the team, the team itself.

Everything is urgent and an emergency in my work. If the manager is spending all their time dealing with crises, there is a bigger problem. It shows a lack of adequate planning. One of the tools we taught in our Effective Management series is the use of the Eisenhower Matrix. (Columbia University Office of Student Support) The most important feature of this tool is to separate the urgent from the non-urgent and the important from the unimportant. The more things that can be dealt with in the not urgent/important quadrant, the more that can be prevented from going to the urgent/important quadrant. It is one way to stay out of crisis mode constantly. This is another aspect of professional leadership training that is vital to the organization of today.

It's all or nothing – either I empower, or I don't. This is what I call "totalizing." It is an easy escape route to taking responsibility for the whole team's success. It is an excuse not to try. If one doesn't look for the opportunity to empower, they won't find it. It's rather clear that different employees may require different forms of empowerment. That doesn't mean it requires too much time or that if everyone doesn't respond appropriately, it shouldn't be tried at all. I have repeated to many clients, "I'm not saying it will be easy; I am saying it will be worth it."

If I ask too many questions, my staff will feel uncomfortable. It depends on the nature of the questions. If they take the form of a test or interrogation, they will not respond well. However, if the questions come from a place of authentic curiosity, they will be more effective. (Milner, 2024) One statement that I have encountered that is similar to this is –" if I ask questions, it will look like I don't know what I am doing." Everyone understands that we don't or can't know everything. Admitting you don't have an answer is actually empowering.

I can add a couple of my own responses. I have heard:

The employees will just take advantage of what they see as permissive. This is a matter of a lack of trust. All too often, I discovered a management style that was directed at those who were misbehaving. This ignored all those who were doing their job. If the leader relies mostly on reward and punishment, the team will seek to avoid punishment and therefore not be creative or engaged.

I am not allowed to do that. Then I want to talk to your supervisor to find out why. I have yet to have an instance where this turned out to be true.

All of these challenges can be addressed with appropriate training, including mentoring. The only way we can break the cycle of poor management resulting in more poor management is to teach better practices and follow up. Some things won't work the first time or may need to be adjusted to meet the situation. Well-developed training programs can go far to make the needed changes and build up better leadership practices.

Chapter 7:
Poor Conflict Skills

While I covered some of this earlier, a more detailed discussion is in order. This is the most common issue I deal with as a consultant. Even in cases where the initial discussion was about morale, most of the time it turned into unhealthy conflict. The truth of the matter is that this really does cause a great deal of misery at work. People behave badly when they are in conflict. It really comes as no surprise if we think about it. We are not taught healthy conflict skills as we go through our developmental years. Most of the time, the only admonition from teachers or parents is "stop fighting." We do learn some basic social skills in grade school, but once children get to middle school and on, there is little in more advanced social skills being taught. Most of us would agree that middle school is generally a jungle. It is pretty clear that the behaviors on social media are rather deplorable. This is largely because the social skills themselves are rather lacking. Consequently, most of us think of conflict in very negative terms. This is because we don't know how to do it.

Let's take a more detailed look at the conflict styles, as described by Killmann. (Kilmann, 2023)

The model developed by Kenneth W. Thomas and Ralph H. Killmann begins with identifying two dimensions, assertiveness and cooperativeness. These are placed on a matrix to present the different styles. Assertiveness is described as the degree to which people are willing to take initiative and force their will upon others. This is a bit different than how I describe assertive communication, which is the effort to balance my needs with yours. In terms of conflict style, however, this makes sense. Perhaps I would tone it down a bit to say the extent to which an individual is willing to advocate for their own needs. The amount of energy used ranges from a high of aggressive to a low of passive. The second dimension of cooperativeness is the degree to which people are willing to work together with others. On the high end, this amounts to a concern for the needs of others. On the low end, this is selfishness. The various conflict styles are then placed on a matrix, as seen in Figure 1.

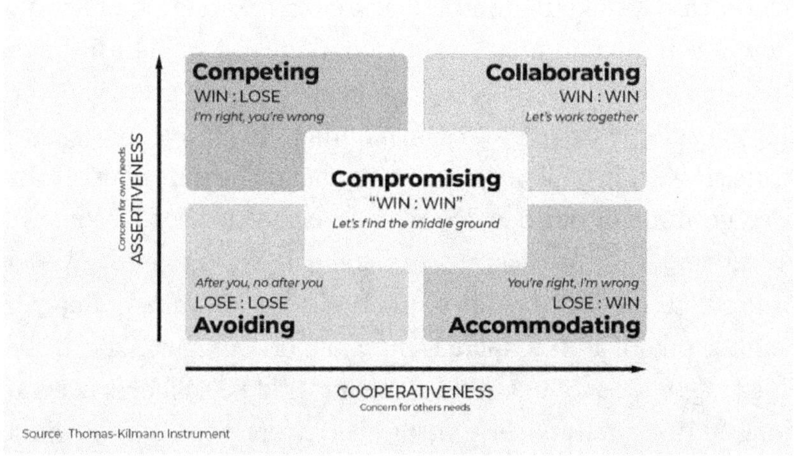

(Kilmann, 2023)Figure 1: Thomas-Kilmann matrix

As can be seen in the matrix, the general idea is how each of the dimensions results in a conflict style. A bit of caution is needed here. This does not mean that a person stays in a particular style. We generally move about this matrix, depending on circumstances. We do, however, have preferred styles. Since this is behavioral, this can change.

The general styles are:

High assertive - low cooperative = Compete

Low assertive – low cooperative = Avoid

Low assertive – high cooperative = Accommodate

High assertive – high cooperative = Collaborate

Moderate assertive – moderate cooperative = Compromise

Notice that each quadrant is labeled in terms of the outcome or goal. So, we can look at each style and foresee what the desired outcome might be. This is how the Kilmann Diagnostics site describes each style:

Competing is assertive and uncooperative—an individual pursues his own concerns at the other person's expense. This is a power-oriented mode in which you use whatever power seems appropriate to win your own position—your ability to argue, your rank, or economic sanctions. Competing means "standing up for your rights," defending a position that you believe is correct, or simply trying to win.

Accommodating is unassertive and cooperative—the complete opposite of competing. When accommodating, the individual neglects his own concerns to satisfy the concerns of the other person; there is an element of self-sacrifice in this mode. Accommodating might take the form of selfless generosity or charity, obeying another person's order when you would prefer not to, or yielding to another's point of view.

Avoiding is unassertive and uncooperative—the person neither pursues his own concerns nor those of the other individual. Thus, he does not deal with the conflict. Avoiding might take the form of diplomatically sidestepping an issue, postponing an issue until a better time, or simply withdrawing from a threatening situation.

Collaborating is both assertive and cooperative—the complete opposite of avoiding. Collaborating involves an attempt to work with others to find a solution that fully satisfies their concerns. It means digging into an issue to pinpoint the underlying needs and wants of the two individuals. Collaborating between two people might take the form of exploring a disagreement to learn from each other's insights or trying to find a creative solution to an interpersonal problem.

Compromising is moderate in both assertiveness and cooperativeness. The objective is to find some expedient, mutually acceptable solution that partially satisfies both parties. It falls intermediate between competing and accommodating. Compromising gives up more than competing but less than accommodating. Likewise, it addresses an issue more directly than avoiding, but does not explore it in as much depth as collaborating. In some situations, compromising might mean splitting the difference between the two positions, exchanging concessions, or seeking a quick middle-ground solution.

Each of us is capable of using all five conflict-handling modes. None of us can be characterized as having a single style of dealing with conflict. But certain people use some modes better than others and, therefore, tend to rely on those modes more heavily than others—whether because of temperament or practice.

Your conflict behavior in the workplace is, therefore, a result of both your personal predispositions and the requirements of the situation in which you find yourself. The Thomas-Kilmann Instrument is designed to measure your use of conflict-handling modes across a wide variety of group and organizational settings. (Kilmann, 2023)

I disagree with only one part of the instrument in which they describe the result of compromise as "win-win." I find that the result is generally more "lose-lose." The truth is that whenever a compromise is chosen, the parties each give up something. This may be an easier way to resolve a conflict, but it is generally short-term. If this is chosen frequently, the parties involved may have a sense of always losing. Claire Canfield describes it as being "mutually miserable." (TedxUSU, 2016) As I noted earlier, we have found that the largest number of people preferred Avoid as a conflict style. This wasn't just a matter of the managers choosing to avoid, but the members of the team, as well. This is largely because conflict is generally seen as something negative. If the experiences we have had with conflict have been unpleasant and unproductive, it would make sense that people want to avoid it. The problem with the strategy is that it can lead to even worse conflict. When I have to intervene in a conflict that has been going on for years, I am just amazed. The amount of time and energy that is wasted on such things is staggering. To be fair, it is understandable if people have not learned how to deal with conflict constructively. Nevertheless, one would think that it should be apparent that such long-term conflicts are not healthy.

To be clear, there is a situation and place where each conflict style is appropriate. Using avoid, for example, is preferred when the issue at hand is very short-term. If the matter isn't going to be relevant tomorrow, then it is just as well to let it go. Compete is appropriate when the issue is genuinely a matter of principle. I do emphasize genuine thought. We have to be clear that something is a matter of values or integrity and not just ego. I have had plenty of occasions where I felt that my integrity was on the line. As a consultant, I have made it clear that my integrity is not for sale. That is a healthy form of competing. Accommodating is appropriate when we really don't have a stake in the issue. If what the other person is doing doesn't really affect me, I really don't need to engage in conflict. Compromise is better when a decision needs to be made fairly quickly. This is especially the case when what I may be ceding is really not that important. Sometimes, that is the hardest thing to recognize. Collaboration is preferred for developing long-term solutions. This does involve commitment on everyone's part to put in the effort. The skill that matters is the wherewithal to select the correct conflict style. Sometimes, it involves moving from one style to another in order to find a solution.

I do need to clarify that avoidance is not necessarily the same as the very common practice of not speaking to each other. This is a classic passive-aggressive strategy that very frequently occurs in conflict in organizations. This may be a matter of avoiding, but it can also be used for the complete strategy as well. It could even be used as part of the accommodation strategy. What matters is the intent of the parties not speaking. If they are using it to get their way, it is the complete approach. If, on the other hand, they are using it to say "let them have their way," it is definitely accommodating. This brings me to one of my surprising discoveries in my work with teams. I was shocked at the number of times I found that adults in organizations were pouting. This is one of the phenomena that led me to reconsider how I see conflict. People are terrible at conflict because they never develop the social skills one would hope to see in adults. One would think that we would understand that we can't always have our way. However, it doesn't seem to be the case. Each time people can have things just as they think they should be, they turn to unhealthy conflict practices. The current political climate supports this hypothesis.

Collaboration is the least used conflict style. This is largely because it is frequently misunderstood. Many people, including consultants and organizational leaders, confuse it with compromise. The difference is both in the process and the outcome. The process is one where the two or more perspectives are shared, without judgment. Then, a search ensues to identify commonalities. Once these are established, the real differences may be addressed. What is most important here is that the parties are not asked to give up anything. Instead, the focus turns to values and how they might be addressed. The way I have described it to clients is that the solution(s) are likely to be found in a "third way." Rather than deciding which of the two ways should prevail, a different alternative is sought. The endpoint is a "win-win" solution.

Through this process, it is far more likely that a long-term solution will be discovered. It requires innovation and open-mindedness. The challenge, of course, is that people need to be taught how to do this. In our culture, we believe that competition is the best way to make progress. While it has and does contribute to some innovations, it is not the best way to arrive at long-term solutions to long-standing conflict issues. It does take considerably more time and commitment on the part of everyone involved. However, it will have greater benefits in the long run. The main reason collaboration is rarely used is that it is misunderstood, and people lack the necessary skills to pull it off. This is also not taught in schools. Until recently, if students collaborated, it was called cheating. Admittedly, it is countercultural, so I will discuss it further in later chapters on suggested reforms.

Generally, our attitude toward conflict is that it is a "zero-sum game." The view is that whatever I win, you lose, and vice versa. Even in the event of accommodation, the perspective is that while I am giving up, it means I lose, and you win. Consequently, the language tends to rely on non-assertive communication. By that, I mean that the idea of balancing my needs with your needs is not adequately considered. The frequent use of "you" statements is very common when there is conflict.

A person might say to their opponent, "You're trying to take over my project."

The key part of this is "you're trying."

It goes right to the intent of the other person. Any time we assume intent on the other person's part, we enter troubling territory. We can never know another's intent. People will naturally react defensively when they hear such statements. Frequently, the "you" word triggers a defensive reaction. In another example, which I have heard used many times, "you have a bad attitude," the likely response is resistance. We don't know anything about another person's attitude. What we can know is the behaviors that we observe, but we can't necessarily identify their cause.

The biggest problem I have witnessed is the failure of leadership to intervene. The prevalence of the avoidance of conflict is one contributor, but not the only one. I have encountered cases where they have actually been told not to intervene. The idea was that the people involved would work things out. This risks creating a long-term, intense conflict situation that will infest the entire team. A recent case that I was asked to help with involved two people on the same team who had been in conflict for eight years! My first question of leadership was why this had been allowed to go on for so long. Their response was that they were told that this was a personal matter and that the work was still getting done. The problem was that it may have been getting done, but it required far more energy than it should have.

The two employees would go to great lengths to avoid one another and would require intermediaries to pass on any communication. This just made no sense. After failing to get the two together to work things out, I recommended that disciplinary action was necessary. My view of discipline may be different than most, however. The goal is to have successful employees, not to fire people. Unfortunately, the managers in this case chose not to take this action. As far as I know, the conflict continues.

One of the most significant challenges in dealing with conflict is that we frequently misidentify what the conflict really concerns. Many times, in my consultations, I have to listen very carefully and probe before I can pinpoint the primary source. Without that, the solutions developed by the team will not work.

The following are the general sources of conflict:

Data: These include things like a lack of information or even misinformation. It could involve different interpretations of the data or even its relevance. It could involve disinformation, which is the intentional distortion or outright lies. However, that indicates a much larger problem.

Values: This includes different lifestyles, ideologies, or world views. It could also include different ways of evaluating the importance or relevance of ideas. In the past decade, this has become a more common source of conflict. Prior to that, the general rule of thumb was not to discuss such things.

Structural: Such conflicts may arise from things like being understaffed or unequal distribution of resources. It could involve the use of time or respect for each other's time. Sometimes, these are a matter of the organization's makeup, hierarchy, or flat structure. This can be a matter of the culture of the team that may run contrary to the task environment.

Interest: Interest conflicts can be a bit harder to identify. They are generally a matter of perception of what counts as influential or even crucial to a person's or team's success. The most common form of this I have seen has to do with procedures.

Relational: This is the crucial area that is most overlooked. What is seen as centered on one of the other sources is actually more about relationships. They can be misidentified as communication issues, for example. The problem isn't necessarily about miscommunication, as it is about either relationship failure or incongruity. There are many ways this is exhibited. Typically, they involve very strong emotions. They can result from stereotypes. This one stands out when it comes to generational conflicts. More often than any other source, I found this to be the one that resulted in a call for intervention. I have become particularly sensitive to watching for this source. Mainly, because it is the one that is overlooked.

To illustrate how misidentification can have such a counterproductive and harmful effect, I turn to my personal journey. In the mid-1990s, I left my position at a university because I felt I had a call to the priesthood, the Catholic kind. When I approached the vocations director of my diocese, he seemed very enthusiastic about the possibility. I filled out all the paperwork and went through some testing and interviews. These were primarily used to identify any psychological issues that could be a problem. I also endured a couple of interviews by a panel of priests. During one of them, there were many questions related to obedience. That should have been a red flag, but I chalked it up to a misunderstanding about me. I told them that I was a veteran of the U. S. Navy and knew quite well how to follow orders, as I had done so for over six years. Apparently, I passed all the screening and moved on with the process.

I was then sent to visit the seminary that the diocese ordinarily sent its candidates. I was not impressed. I found the place to be directed far more at younger men, and the classes to be overly simplistic. I was a bit surprised, to be honest. I didn't want to come across as arrogant, but these were supposed to be at the graduate level, and that was not my impression. I was particularly struck by several inadequate answers to questions about historical events in a class that I attended. When I expressed my disappointment to the bishop, he suggested that I visit a different seminary. This one was designed for "second career vocations" a nice euphemism for old farts.

When I visited this seminary back east, it seemed to be much more appropriate for me. So off I went, leaving home and family. At first, things seem to be going well. My classmates were decent guys. They even elected me as their class president. I should have known better, but that's another story. The classes were mostly decent, approaching graduate level, but brought out some good information. There were a couple of classes that were rather dreadful, but I expected that. I did have a couple of points where I had some differences with colleagues. These were mostly about values or structure. That did not trouble me.

After our Christmas break, things took a sudden turn for the worse. It began with my second semester of philosophy. Unlike the first semester, where I generally kept my mouth shut because I didn't want to come off as a showoff, I decided to participate in the discussion. The professor, a very nice older Jesuit priest, asked to speak to me after class. He asked me why I was in his class. I told him that it was required. He suggested that I talk to the academic dean and tell him I didn't need to take the class. I did as he suggested, and the request was denied. I told the professor that I had to take the class. He was disappointed for me and then asked if I would do him a favor and explain deconstructionism to him. In exchange, I didn't need to take any of the tests.

Apparently, that struck a nerve with the seminary leadership. A couple of weeks later, the academic dean pulled me aside and told me that I should stop trying to take over his class. I had no idea what he was talking about since I never spoke in his class once. Frankly, I never had the opportunity to say anything. In class, all he did was read from the book. I walked away completely confused, but assured him that I had no such intention. Only a week later, in another class, I was confronted with the same thing. This was the homiletics class. After one of the guys finished giving his sample homily, my friend asked me what I thought. I briefly said I thought it was pretty good. The professor looked right at me and said, "This is my class, I don't need you taking it over." I was stunned. It was way too much of a coincidence that the same accusation came up again. This really put me into a tailspin. After a couple more confrontations with the priests in charge, I discerned that I was clearly in the wrong place. I left in mid-semester. This is something I had never done before. I was very disappointed and really had no idea what I had done to merit these confrontations. The bishop was very unhappy with me and lectured me on not being able to finish the program. I came home with nothing, including a job.

During the next couple of years, I worked various odd jobs and then got a job building fences from a friend. It was hard work, but it was probably good for me to figure out where I was headed. During this time, I struggled mightily with this continued sense of calling to the priesthood. A friend asked me if I had considered any of the religious orders. A religious order is a different path to the priesthood. Order priests are not attached to a particular diocese, and generally they live in community. After a brief search, I found an order that was suited to my needs. They emphasized that they valued my current skills and did not want to remake me into something I was not. So, off I went again, leaving everything behind. The experience with the order was mostly positive. The one issue that did arise was related to the fact that I have children. They hadn't experienced that before and didn't understand my need to remain connected to my children and grandchildren. Sometimes, they would tell me that they had left their families. I explained that leaving parents and siblings is quite different from leaving children. They could not understand that I would always be a dad. After four years, this issue became rather untenable. That was more my fault than theirs, if it could be called a fault. My daughter was struggling as a single mother of three. I decided that my first vocation was as a father. So, I left the order and asked if I could complete my studies for the diocese. At first, I was received very well. I only had one more year of seminary to complete. So, it was a good deal for the diocese in terms of expense.

During the summer that year, I met the new bishop. He seemed rather cold to my candidacy, but I figured that was just because he didn't know me. Then, he started stating different reasons for not wanting to ordain me. This changed with each of our meetings. First, he said he was hesitant to ordain older guys. Then he was apprehensive about guys with families (meaning children). Then, he wasn't enthusiastic about guys coming from an order. At one point, he intimated that he assumed that I would expect to work at the diocesan college because of my credentials. In each case, I assured him that I had no expectations beyond what any priest would have. While not ideal, things seemed to be going along smoothly until disaster hit. One of my younger siblings sent a letter to the bishop accusing me of molesting her when she was a child. This was the first I had heard of this.

I was called to the chancery (diocesan headquarters) to meet with the bishop. When I entered the room, the bishop was there with two priests. I was pretty sure this was trouble. He informed me that he had received the letter, accusing me of abuse. I had no idea what he was talking about. I was not allowed to see the letter for myself. I acknowledged that I had naturally made mistakes in the past, but they were not sexual abuse or even involved her. He said that he would initiate an investigation with an" independent" party. I just had to consent. I was not comfortable with this since this was the problem with the whole sex abuse scandal. If they thought I had committed this crime, they should report it to the local authorities.

After a few days of reflection, I declined the investigation because it would unnecessarily cause chaos in my family. Shortly after, I was informed that a person from Child Protective Services (CPS) was investigating me. The result of the investigation was that there was no case. I learned that this alleged incident happened when my sibling was 13. That gave me solid evidence that the incident could not have taken place. At that time, I lived over 900 miles away from her. I presented the evidence to the bishop, both in the conclusion of the CPS investigation and a document showing that I was stationed elsewhere. He said it did not matter, and he would tell any other bishop not to ordain me. He was upset that I did not consent to his investigation. I was devastated.

Subsequent reflection over the next few months, I realized that I had misunderstood the conflict. The issue in each of the confrontations was not what I had assumed. With the first seminary, it was not that I was being arrogant in saying the classes were not at the graduate level. With the second seminary for older men, it was not that I was trying to control their classes. With the bishop, it was not all the reasons that he stated or even the final one. The real issue was relational. I had assumed that the issues were structural or even values. They were not. The issue was tied to the expectation of the relationship I would have with the church. I was expected to be totally compliant. Suppose I had been told that in the beginning in clear terms, I would have saved myself ten years of frustration. I know that I am non-compliant. This is not a matter of having the ability to follow orders. It is a matter of determination for me what orders are necessary to follow. This goes to show that this is a very hard lesson to learn. A key step in conflict is correctly identifying the source.

The problem of poor conflict skills also goes to the heart of failure to build relationships. Most of us know that relationship building can be very difficult. One of the reasons for this is our aversion to conflict. People are bound to have different perspectives and expectations. When these clash, the result is perceived as conflict, but in negative terms. The self-deceptive practice of offense-taking also comes into play. It makes sense, then, that we don't do relationship-building very well and that this is one of the key causes of dysfunction in organizations. Admittedly, when I speak of the number of assholes in the workplace, I am describing how we tend to perceive others. It is worth remembering that the manager or colleague who is acting poorly in our eyes goes through the same mental processing. It's not so much a matter that they are bad people. It is more likely that they lack the skills to navigate human interaction.

Chapter 8:
Bureaucracy

Bureaucracy is not about large organizations, and it is not about government. The current form of bureaucracy is found in public and private entities. It is a uniquely industrial form. Of course, there were bureaucracies in earlier times, but they were generally quite different from the industrial ones. The Romans had a large organization, but a key feature was the level of autonomy given to local jurisdictions. Most of what was done in Rome's name depended on the personality of the local governor. This was partially due to the difficulty with communication. The main function of the bureaucracy was to procure material for the empire, especially the military. The Middle Ages also had a form of bureaucracy, which was mainly found in the church. This was primarily to maintain orthodoxy and collect funds.

The difference in the modern form of bureaucracy is that it has nothing to do with a particular person, family, or function. As described by Max Weber, it is a specific form of organization. It is completely reliant on the rules. It is also focused on positions and not people. I will not repeat the first part of the description that I wrote earlier. However, the centrality of structure is crucial. His description is very elegant in its completeness and logic. It is clearly a rational model. If we look at the second part of his description, the image becomes even clearer. The official is assumed to be on a career path, i.e., working in the bureau for life. He is also expected to be appointed by a higher authority. (Weber, Essays in Sociology -- translated by Gerth and Mills, 1946) All of it is designed to make the bureaucracy stable. The idea was to avoid the chaos of shifts in governance by changes in leadership. Previously, organizations were directed by those in the nobility or the owners of businesses. Organizations had become so large that this was untenable.

The most important thing to remember is that this structure is intended to be impersonal. This is made abundantly clear by Robert Merton:

A formal, rationally organized social structure involves clearly defined patterns of activity in which, ideally, every series of actions is functionally related to the purposes of the organization. In such an organization there is integrated series of offices, of hierarchized statuses, in which are inhere a number of obligations and privileges closely defined by limited and specific rules. Each of these offices contains an area of imputed competence and responsibility. Authority, the power of control which derives from an acknowledged status, *inheres in the office and not in the particular person who performs the official role.* (emphasis mine) (Merton, 1957)

This is directly tied to the industrial concept that organizations are like machines. Everyone has a particular role and is replaceable. It is intentionally isolating in many ways. The only relationship that matters is the one immediately above or below each bureaucrat. One might argue that just because the organization is designed in such a way doesn't mean that people will not be personal. That is not my experience. Researchers have found that the nature of the institution has a very direct impact on its members.

It is likely that social structures 'effect,' influence, or 'shape' institutions (rules, conventions, norms, values, and customs), which, in turn, cause the emergence of a habitus [organizational culture] that, in some sense, 'reflects' or 'expresses' these social structures. Social structures have a causal role to play in generating the habitus, but only indirectly via institutions and, I might add, organizations. (Fleetwood, 2008)

It is not that institutions have not played a positive role. They certainly have done so.

[Institutions]…are the reason why people have been able to organize in society, work in groups, and live in large communities, and so on. Without institutions, people would not have been able to adopt clear behaviors that would inspire safety, because each of us would have followed his [sic] own instincts and prejudices… The institutions came up with the solution of restricting the behavior of all members of society, seeking compliance with all the proposed rules, and punishing non-compliance to ensure non-deviation from the general rules formulated to ensure the safety and welfare of all. (Gavrol, 2021)

The problem is the particular form of institution that operates today. We continue to operate under the industrial model of bureaucracy. This is actually a misfit in today's postindustrial society.

In 1977, Ralph Hummel published *The Bureaucratic Experience,* in which he describes the nature of bureaucracies in modern times. (Hummel, 2007) He has published revisions up until 2007. Hummel argues that bureaucracy is dehumanizing as it focuses on efficiency at the expense of other human values. He emphasizes that what the bureaucrat normally deals with are cases instead of people. His thesis continues to hold true today. This is entirely consistent with what I argue here. The bureaucratic environment is one in which relationship building and flexibility are actively discouraged. Bear in mind that this is not just a matter of public organizations. These same principles are in play in the private sector as well. That is one reason that many large corporations can carry out mass layoffs and outsourcing so readily. Some have gone further to describe bureaucracy and its incumbent behaviors as a pathology. (Aupperle, 1984)

As shown in Figure 1, the idea is that people in bureaucratic organizations tend to get caught in the cycle of rule-making and de-personalizing.

Our concept of pathology relates to the deliberate shunning of learning opportunities, whatever the reason. We shall therefore consider the behavior of a management system B to be "pathological" when B becomes unwilling to guide its containing system S through an adaptive-learning mode of behavior. Symptoms of such a pathology exist when B prevents S from questioning its norms or assumptions so as to develop more effectively, or, more visibly, when B obstructs changes or improvements in S. (Aupperle, 1984)

As the chart shows, the arrangement of bureaucracy is self-reinforcing. The process begins with both the development of the rules and the changing of people into positions. From there, individual success is achieved by supporting the system. Rare is the person who moves up in the organization who defies the rules or questions procedures. The more senior people, especially, develop what Hummel called the "bureaucratic personality." (Hummel, 2007) While the system is inherently rational, it is not necessarily a problem solver. The rules are extensive and largely rigid. Consequently, it is more likely that the behavior of the organization is to be more like solutions looking for a problem. Cohen, March, and Olsen refer to this in their so-called "garbage can theory" of organizational choice. (Cohen, 1972) This results in much of the effort seeming to lead nowhere. Meetings are unnecessarily long and frequently result in little or no decision-making.

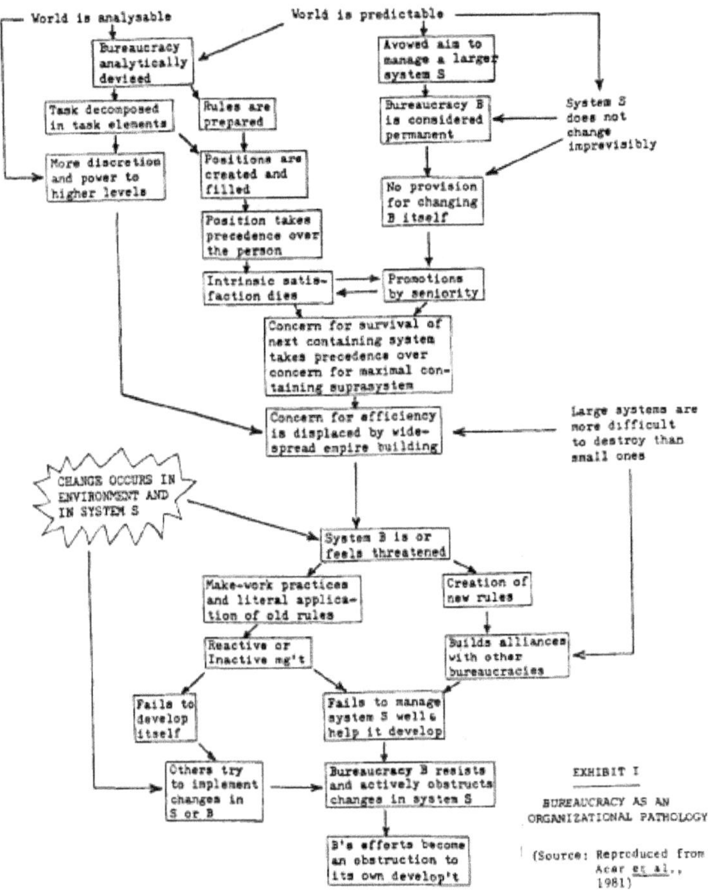

Figure 2: Bureaucracy as pathology (Aupperle, 1984)

The interesting thing about a pathology is that most people are unaware that they are in it. In many cases, they are contributing to it unintentionally. Even in their perceived resistance, they enable the pathology to continue. That is because when they resist, the bureaucracy will create more rules to correct it. Generally, those who are "just doing their job" get immersed in it. They take on the language of the bureaucracy. Over time, they adopt the organization's "sense-making." That is, they see problems and challenges in the way that the organization does. It is highly unusual for novel approaches to arise because the members of the organization have incorporated the logic of the agency or company. (Weick K. E., 1993) The sad thing is that this pathology is a huge part of the reason so many of the employees are miserable. The model itself is centered on being impersonal, even though it is made up of people.

The bureaucratic model itself is a primary source of all the problems that I have discussed at this point. Since the model stresses the idea of positions and not people, it actively discourages relationship building. I very frequently encounter leaders who discourage any personal relationships. The focus on hierarchy naturally leads to forms of arrogance.

The belief is that the further one moves up the hierarchy, the more intelligent and capable they are. I am sure most of us have discovered how common it is that this is simply not true. The need to have multiple layers of accountability and rule enforcement undermines the ability to develop trust. In fact, the model openly emphasizes the need to be very wary of everyone around us. The many layers of hierarchy and the need to project authority result in a lack of transparency.

The people at the top of the hierarchy tend to believe that they must constantly be the keepers of "the vision" and inspiration. The entire bureaucratic model is premised on the illusion of control. The irony is that the more emphasis there is on control, the less control one will have. The stress on control and a lack of transparency lend themselves to untrained managers. To survive in bureaucracy, or more to the point, to climb the ladder, one must be committed to rule enforcement. This is how those who move up succumb to the pathology. The aim of the model is to limit the role of human passion, which leads to poor conflict skills. When we seek to limit the natural way humans function, with emotions and passion, we only undermine the tools needed to work through conflict.

Another significant factor is the manner in which decisions are made. There is a firm belief that the process is rational. This suggests that the only considerations are facts and figures. Most of the decision-making models tend to be quantitative. The common adage is that "the data sets you free." (Payne, 2014) Does it really? This sounds quite reasonable and even falls into the category of common sense. Sometimes, the problem with common sense is that it is not examined. Data can certainly be helpful. However, we have to know that it is valid and reliable. Does the data accurately reflect reality? Data taken out of context can convince us of something that is not exactly true. We are attached to the rational model of decision-making, believing that it is more objective. If it is more objective, then the decisions will be the correct ones. One would think that if that were true, we would be making better decisions than we do. Part of the problem is that objectivity is an illusion. In any decision model that is driven by data, the first question is. How was it acquired? I have done enough survey research to find out that this data is anything but objective. It relies so much on self-reporting that it tells us right away that it is largely a guess. People are not usually clear on their viewpoints or even their self-awareness.

Even when we apply highly structured quantitative models, we are at considerable risk of a poor decision. For example, one commonly used model is the matrix or decision tree. In this model, a set of alternatives is considered. The possible "states of nature" are applied to each alternative. These include the probability that the particular state (e.g., the winter will be mild, average, or severe) with an estimate of the cost or gain. There are several issues here that can dramatically influence the ultimate value of the decision. The first is the fact that the number of options considered is usually very limited. The second is the number of variables associated with the state of nature. Third, the probabilities used can be a stretch, especially if the model assumes that the past is a predictor of the future. These models may be handy for visualizing a decision event, but reliance on them can and does present many problems.

The issue that stands out is that these quantitative models are frequently the wrong tool for the decision environment. The best tool for understanding this is called "The Cynefin Framework" (Snowden, 2007). It is important to know that this is a framework and not a model. The essential idea is that the method of decision-making is tied to the complexity of the problem. Another way of putting it is that there are different search procedures that apply. The framework is made up of five domains defined by the nature of the relationship between cause and effect. Four of these are simple (sometimes called either obvious or routine), complicated, complex, and chaotic. These require decision-makers to diagnose a situation and to act in contextually appropriate ways. (Snowden, 2007) The fifth one is a disorder, when it is unclear which of the other four domains is predominant. Figure 1 presents the graphic depiction of the framework; the center of the figure is the area of disorder.

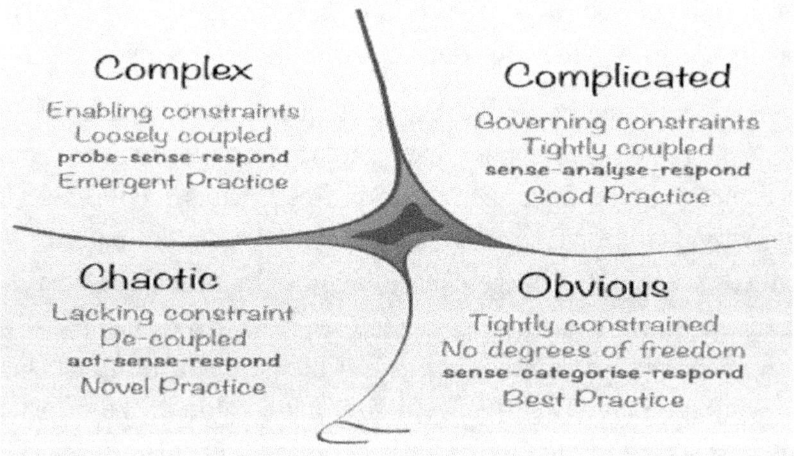

Figure 3: The Cynefin Framework (Source: The Canadian Association for the Club of Rome

The following describes the different domains of the framework:

Obvious. These are situations that are rather routine, and the cause is known. In bureaucracies, they are typically approached through standard operating procedures. For example, if a person needs to renew their driver's license and there are no changes or unusual elements, the same process is used. The driver submits and signs a form, a photo is taken, the fee is paid, and the license is issued. Another example is in the medical profession. If a child comes to the emergency room with a broken arm, the treatment is obvious and doesn't require any research. The process is sense-categorize-respond. The medical professional identifies the arm as broken, recognizes the treatment for a fracture, and follows the normal procedure. The outcome falls under the general category of best practice.

Complicated. Sometimes, the problem is not so straightforward. There may be conditions that do not meet the obvious standards. This brings us into the complicated domain. Maybe the person needing to renew the driver's license has had a name change or has let their current license lapse for over a year. This requires more thought and expertise on the part of the agent. In the case of an urgent care clinic, if a person comes in with what may be a heart attack, the diagnosis is far more complicated and requires the expertise of a specialist to determine the proper treatment. The response then is to sense, analyze, and respond. It would be a mistake in these cases to simply apply the same standardized procedure. The outcome falls under the category of good practice.

Complex. In still other cases, the situation may present far more complications that will yield the same result with the particular responses. This complex domain requires more investigation and more trial-and-error approaches. In the driver's license case, the person has physical limitations, combined with legal requirements for accommodations. This requires more extensive exploration and even some creative processes to be certain that the correct response is provided. In the medical area, the treatment of diabetes is particularly complex. Individual patients don't respond to the same treatments. It is not uncommon for health care providers to try multiple approaches until the right combination is discovered. (Gray, 2017)

I had experienced this with my own health issue. I kept having episodes of severe abdominal pain. The doctors were able to stop the pain each time, but were unable to diagnose the issue. I even traveled to the Mayo Clinic, and they offered what they thought was the issue. It turned out that they were wrong. Ultimately, my allergist guessed at the source of the problem. The strategy was to try a particular treatment the next time I had an event. If the treatment worked, then we had a diagnosis. The process for the decision is probe, sense, respond. The experts need to try things until something works. The outcome falls under the category of emergent practice.

Chaotic. There are many occasions where chaos ensues. The challenges have no apparent solution and require immediate response. These can be crisis situations that don't allow for considerable reflection and exploration for a solution. Car accidents, riots, or natural disasters fall into this domain. This requires on-the-spot decisions that are made on the fly. The process is act, sense, respond. The result is a novel practice. The essential goal is to move back into either complex or complicated environments.

Disorder. There are times when situations become downright mysterious. When situations fall into disorder, there are no apparent responses. It may also be called the dark confusion domain. It is hard to see when this domain applies. "Here, multiple perspectives jostle for prominence, factional leaders argue with one another, and cacophony rules." (Snowden, 2007) The way out of this realm is to break down the situation into appropriate parts and apply the domains that will work for each part. The last thing any group wants is to stay in this situation.

One of the particularly interesting parts of the Cynefin framework is the relationship between the obvious and the chaotic domains. The caution is that if a person or organization stubbornly remains in the obvious domain, there is a high risk of falling into the chaotic one. This is particularly problematic for bureaucracies. The strong attachment to the rules and standard operating procedures may cause the decision makers to apply the wrong response to conditions more and more frequently. This is a clue to where we find ourselves now. I will expand on this shortly in this chapter.

There are those who defend bureaucracy as the best means to organize. The most common argument is that the structure of bureaucracy dampens the impact of human passion in making decisions. This is largely a matter of wishful thinking. Even in the cases of routine decisions, human beings involve passion or values. One of the biggest misconceptions is that we can be rational beings. We cannot. We are emotional and relational beings, but not rational. If we were rational beings, we would not use the explanation of "we've always done it this way" when asked about certain procedures. This just shows that we don't know why we do it a certain way. More to the point, it shows an emotional attachment to the procedure. Rationality would immediately refute such an explanation as illogical. This is another sign of the weakness of the model.

Some of the defenders of bureaucracy claim that its resilience shows that it is the most appropriate organizational form. Over the years, critics have laid out the problems created by bureaucracy. The defenders argue that the organizations have responded to those criticisms and made the needed adjustments.

Consecutive waves of criticism have bruised and battered the bureaucratic governance paradigm, leading to drastic changes in both content and scope that can be studied by analyzing shifting politico-organizational storylines (Christensen, 2003) and the introduction of competing and coexisting governance paradigms to be studied using a configurational approach (Monteiro & Adler, 2022). Hence, if bureaucracy has survived the persistent attacks, it is due to the work of the ideational robustness strategies that have adapted and innovated the bureaucratic governance paradigm, thus allowing the supporters of bureaucracy to insist on its continued relevance. (Sorensen, 2024)

First, it is interesting that the authors apply the term "paradigm" to the bureaucratic model. It depends on how one uses the term. In recent years, the term has been misused. The idea of paradigms was elevated by Thomas Kuhn in his book *The Structure of Scientific Revolutions.* (Kuhn, 1996) While the bureaucratic model is within the Rational paradigm, it does not stand as a paradigm itself. Kuhn's idea of a paradigm describes it as a result of an exemplary text or body of work. These exemplars set the stage for the practice of science, suggesting that there are certain ways to analyze phenomena. In the case here, the paradigm is the Rational work described by Max Weber. Bureaucracy is but one aspect of this paradigm. Weber describes it as an "iron cage of rationality" (Baehr, 2001). What Sørensen and Torfing describe is bureaucracies, hence the Rational model, responding to anomalies. Kuhn identified this process as an accumulation of anomalies that, at a critical point, bring about a paradigm shift. (Kuhn, 1996) So one could easily interpret the responses to criticisms of bureaucracy as the anomalies. This also suggests that the paradigm shift from Rationalism is upon us.

This brings us to focus on what is happening currently. It is abundantly clear that people are increasingly dissatisfied with the impact of large organizations. This is not just with government bureaucracies. There is an equally increasing pressure mounting against huge corporations. This is much more than the usual grousing about government and business. The dynamics are much more intense. The result is an increasing rise of right-wing movements, alongside demands for better opportunities. In so many ways, the expectations of the larger populations just don't make sense. The same people who complain about big government want the government to do more for them. Those who feel victimized by the shifting economy turn to the leaders of that economy to rescue them. The resistance to science and universities suggests that people are less interested in facts and disciplined thinking. The presence of abundant information has not led to people being more informed. Rather, it has resulted in more people having their own facts. All of this suggests that a major shift is about to take place. Half of the population is striving for an imagined past. The other half is pushing for an unknown future. Historically, this indicates a major shift is underway. The challenge is that the system, which is in its final stage, becomes its most aggressive. These are huge concerns.

I focus on organizations because they demonstrate the tectonic shifts occurring in most developed nations. Bureaucracy, at least the one premised on the Rational paradigm, is a glaring example of these strains. The alienation that exists in our organizations is a symptom of broader strains worldwide. Zygmunt Bauman describes this trend:

Ours times of transition insofar as the old structures are falling apart or have been dismantled, while no alternative structures with an equal institutional hold are about to be put in their place. It is as if the moulds into which human relationships were poured to acquire shape have now themselves been thrown into a melting pot. Deprived of such moulds, all patterns of relationships become as suspicious as they are uncertain and vulnerable, amenable to challenge and open to negotiation. (Bauman, The Individualized Society, 2001)

Bauman further argues that we have become so individualized and alienated from each other that long-term relationship building has become nearly impossible. There is more of a utility to relationships than sincerity and risk-taking. Others have pointed out the same problems. Robert Putnam, in his book *Bowling Alone*, described how association with community groups had declined. (Putnam, 2000) The bottom line is that our current organizational structures are unsustainable. The workplace has to change in dramatically different ways. Organizations are supposed to be places of creativity and problem-solving. The old industrial structure undermines our ability to do that. That is why they are so dysfunctional, and so many people are miserable in their jobs.

Chapter 9: Education

One of the most crucial elements of how we organize and how we behave in organizations is the way we are educated. The current system of education is well-suited to the industrial or Rational model. Throughout our K-12 years and our postsecondary experiences, we are taught to follow routines and operate individually. However, this is not appropriate for the postindustrial era. Many of the problems I have described are supported by the current educational paradigm. This is not sustainable. Our organizational difficulties are directly related to our social, cultural, and political challenges. These, in turn, are tied to our education.

Very early on in our K-12 education, we see the roots of our issues. Depending on the location (i.e., school district), the orientation to standardized behavior begins. Children are taught that they must conform to particular rules and learning expectations. I had a personal experience that demonstrates this well. My grandson was in the first grade. One morning, I had an extremely difficult time taking him to school. He was terrified to the point that he had to be physically dragged out of the car. I was shocked because it is more common for first graders to love school. So, we set up a meeting with the school staff to find out what was happening. The teacher explained that he was frequently uncooperative in class. He would finish his assignments much earlier than the other students. So, while he was waiting, he would get fidgety and try to find something else to do. I responded that it was no surprise. He was already reading chapter books, and I am sure he is bored. Perhaps she should give him something else to read. The teacher and the principal both dismissed this immediately, stating that all of the students had to do the same thing. Then, another teacher complained that he had a problem during the lunch break. Apparently, the expectation was that the children had to be in a single file line and only look forward, with no talking. My daughter and I were shocked, to say the least. We had five more meetings with the school (that grew to seven staff members) with absolutely no progress. In fact, it got worse. The main focus of the school was control. The next year, we decided he would be home-schooled.

At first, I thought this was an isolated case, unique to the particular school. As I observed other schools and the material being used in schools of education at universities, I came to realize that this was not the case. Teacher education is surprisingly rigid. In the programs I observed, the tendency was for the candidates to be teachers were the lower qualified (based on admission requirements and the standards used to complete the program). To begin with, students are grouped based on their age, regardless of their competencies. My grandson's case points to the fallacy here. He did not belong in the first grade in terms of his cognitive competence. This led to incredible frustration for him and the school. Other children were not ready for first grade, even though they were the standard age. More effort is needed to establish each child's developmental level prior to placement in a class.

Little to no consideration is given to the emotional level of the students. Even though my grandson was cognitively ready, he was not ready emotionally. This added to the difficulty of the situation. The fact that he was clearly traumatized by the experience speaks volumes. Home schooling was the proper fit for him as he had the opportunity to continue his cognitive development and the time to mature emotionally. It is clear that this is another problem with the current industrial model. Home schooling should not be the only option. It worked for him because his parents were both highly educated and were committed to his growth. Not all households have the kind of resources or background to accomplish this. Consequently, public or private schools are still essential, or we will preserve the intergenerational disadvantage.

School programs are driven by the curriculum and not by the learning needs of the students. Centralized education authorities, be it state or local, lay out what every child must learn. While some fundamentals are necessary, e.g., reading and basic math, not all the classes are needed by all the students. Many children will likely go into the trades. Algebra is not necessary for their success. We have all witnessed the high levels of frustration experienced by students who are not strong in math. One of the most common complaints I have heard are those who struggled with geometry. While some basic knowledge of geometry is necessary for many occupations, proofs and trigonometry are generally not. It is appropriate to develop critical thinking skills and citizenship, but the focus should be on what is needed for each student.

Standardized tests play an outsized role in the delivery and content of the curriculum. Since so much is at stake when it comes to test scores, the schools find themselves in a position of "teaching to the test" instead of developing cognitive skills. This became a much larger problem with the publication of *A Nation at Risk* in 1983. (United States National Commission on Excellence in Education, 1983) The report expressed alarm at the declining test scores of U.S. students, compared to those around the globe. The claim was that the test scores had declined by over 20 points between 1960 and 1982. This resulted in a concerted effort nationwide to bring up the scores. School districts were sanctioned if the scores fell below an expected level of competency. This included financial penalties. Naturally, school districts responded accordingly. Considerable effort was dedicated to preparation for the tests. Many schools even had special classes in test-taking skills. Subsequent efforts, including *No Child Left Behind*, from the George W. Bush administration and those from the Barack Obama administration, added resources and incentives to improve test scores. The problem is that the alarm was based on questionable analysis by the commission. First, one thing that was not recognized is that the U. S. was testing all the students.

Most of the other countries did not test all their students. They only tested students who were designated for postsecondary education. Second, they did not take into consideration that during the time in question (1960-1983), more students were being tested who came from disadvantaged circumstances as a result of civil rights legislation. Adding minorities, students from poor districts, and immigrants brought the overall scores down. However, when the scores were examined by demographic groups, the scores actually went up a bit. (Kamenetz, 2018)

Even though we have known about the concept of different intelligences for over 40 years, little consideration is given to the differences. One of the most influential theorists of multiple intelligences was Howard Gardner in 1983. (Gardner, 1983) Gardner included the standard cognitive abilities (or intelligences) of verbal fluency and mathematical reasoning. He also included kinesthetic (movement), music, interpersonal, and intrapersonal. To this set of competencies, we can add Goleman's emotional intelligence. Goleman purports that the elements of emotional intelligence include: self-awareness, self-regulation, motivation, empathy, and social skills. (Goleman, Working with Emotional Intelligence, 1998) Unfortunately, very little attention is paid to these different forms of intelligence. Instead, students are expected to learn the same way. I know in my own experience as a student in high school, the way I was required to learn was completely outside my type of intelligence. I must confess that I was a disaster in high school, barely making it through.

In addition to the failure to adequately take into consideration the different intelligences, the schools generally don't allow for different problem-solving strengths. Kolbe identifies the difference that we find in how we strive and problem-solve. (Kolbe, Powered by Instinct: 5 Rules for Trusting Your Guts, 2004) She describes what she calls "action modes," which combine to form our *modus operandi* or method of operating. Within the four action modes, there are ranges from those who initiate in strength to those who counteract. (Kolbe, Pure Instinct: the M.O. of High Performance People and Teams, 2004).

This is an important consideration when it comes to education. If a student goes about solving a problem in a different manner than others, or more to the point, than the way being taught, they will struggle to satisfy the expectations of the teacher. Personally, when I look back at my struggles in high school, this was the main issue. My style tends to be non-compliant and to simplify complex concepts. I do not do well with rote memorization. This caused many major challenges in so-called objective tests and in following specific steps in math problems. When I went to college years later, I found that I was very comfortable with multiple answers and being creative in my analysis.

There is minimal effort dedicated to teaching relationship building. In the early years, grades 1-5 teachers will teach basic skills of how to get along with others in their classrooms. Most of this is a matter of telling them not to fight. This does not usually include teaching ways to deal with conflict constructively, however. Rather, it is an admonition to stop fighting. Students are also taught about taking their turns and when it is proper to speak up. These are rules directed at maintaining some order in the classroom. When it comes to understanding other children, especially in their differences, little is done. When the students get to middle school, I think it is well known that it becomes a jungle in terms of how the kids relate to one another. These pre-teens and teens are finding their own way in terms of belonging.

This results in a kind of sorting process of those who are in and out. I can certainly acknowledge that teachers and staff will have a great deal of difficulty intervening in these interactions. Most of it takes place outside of the classroom. However, it sets the stage for dysfunction in organizations later in life. It would be prudent to develop more comprehensive experiences where these behaviors can be addressed. This has become even more important in the current era of social media. It will necessarily go back to the schools of education in preparing teachers. I have personally witnessed poor social skills among the teachers themselves. It is time to take this more seriously.

Related to the lack of social competencies, the schools generally don't teach collaboration skills. In the organizations of today, collaboration is much more important. In school, the overall trend is to discourage collaboration. Much of the time, it is considered cheating. We continue to focus on individual assignments and evaluations. Consequently, the students have a very difficult time knowing how to work with others in a more of a group setting. I was able to observe this firsthand as a professor for graduate studies. When I announced the expectations of group projects, the students were quite resistant. They expressed concerns about being evaluated based on the performance of their team. They anticipated that someone on their team would not carry their weight. My response was that they needed to recognize that working with a team would be an expectation in their work lives. I spent considerable time teaching them how to navigate the difficulties of working with others. It became rather obvious that the resistance to working on teams was deeply rooted and began with their K-12 experiences. In my consultations, I have found this to be a huge problem. The one place where this must be addressed is in the primary and secondary levels of education.

For all of the above reasons, and many others, what we have is students who dislike school. Learning should be a positive experience. Yet, what we have is an outdated, grueling experience for students and teachers alike. One just needs to notice the excitement when school lets out for summer or for a snow day. We clearly need substantial reform. (James, 2024) We need to move from 19th and 20th-century practices to accommodate the profound changes of the 21st century:

Much has been written about the inability of nineteenth and twentieth century education structures, approaches, and pedagogies to meet the demands of twenty-first century realities [21-23]. However, as societal norms and technologies continue to shift, the inability of current educational models to respond becomes ever more apparent. There is an urgent need to address the limitations of K12 education [5,10]. Despite the pockets of excellence and transformative teaching and learning happening in schools today, the fundamental pedagogical structures of how we organize education have proven to be deeply resistant to transformation and have remained virtually unchanged for over a century. Entering the nineteenth year of the twenty-first century without having realized substantive, scalable transformation further reflects the pedantic nature of our current educational structures and learning environments. (Patrick Howard, 2019).

This rigidity is directly tied to our clinging to the Rational model. Essentially, the belief is that these were effective methods in the past, so they will continue to be so. Unfortunately, that is simply not the case. We are not preparing people for the same culture or the same workplace.

Higher education presents many of the same issues as K-12. Degree plans are still rather rigid and emphasize individual effort as opposed to team projects. They also do little to help with social skills. There is plenty of evidence that a university education prepares graduates for the world of work as it exists today:

Another study found that nearly three-quarters (73%) of U. S. employers report difficulty finding graduates with essential soft skills, including critical thinking, effective communication, and active listening [9]. A comparative analysis of college graduates and skills-based hires indicated that the former were less proficient in adaptability, intellectual curiosity, communication, collaboration, strategic and critical thinking, and interpersonal relationship building [10] (Friedman, 2025)

It is clear that our postsecondary institutions are not serving our students well. There is every reason to believe that this is closely related to both clinging to old practices and misdirection of resources.

These findings emphasize a pressing need for higher education institutions to reassess and potentially redesign their curricula to better align with the evolving demands of the modern workplace. The disconnect between education and employability must be addressed. (Friedman, 2025)

The areas where graduates need to improve are the same ones that contribute to dysfunctional organizations. Fewer than half of employers believe college graduates are "very well prepared" in the skills they regard as most important for success, including the ability to work effectively in teams (48 percent), critical thinking skills (39 percent), the ability to analyze and interpret data (41 percent), and application of knowledge and skills in real-world settings (39 percent). (Finley, 2021) What has changed is not the way postsecondary education delivers its material. The real change is what is expected of the graduates. This applies to the workplace as well as the communities. Universities are not exclusively job training sites. Their mission is to prepare people to contribute to the well-being of the community. If we look closely at the concerns of the employers, we can easily see how these are also the needs of the community.

Universities and colleges have taken on too much of a business model of operating. This has come about as a result of the spread of neoliberalism. This is a philosophical and political model built on the premise that everything can be viewed in terms of how it contributes to the economy. According to the Encyclopedia Britannica, this is an ideology and policy model that emphasizes the value of free market competition. This includes the belief in sustained economic growth as a means of human progress. It advocates less government intervention and the freedom of trade and capital. This is related to what is considered classical liberalism only in that it seeks greater freedom and a reduction in inequality.

Universities exemplify this in many ways in recent decades. The most obvious way is that the institutions spend a great deal of energy on recruiting students. The motivation behind this is for the advancement of the institution. One observable aspect of this is how much of the university's resources are dedicated to student services. The campuses now include apartment-style dormitories, food courts, and elaborate athletic/recreational facilities. Relatively fewer resources are dedicated to academics. In many cases, this also results in the students being identified as customers. I have experienced this myself. Students have approached me as if they were entitled to consideration for leniency. They would threaten to go to the dean or other staff members and complain about my unwillingness to give in to their demands. One accused me of "lording your degrees over me. I had to explain to students on a regular basis that I was not interested in negotiating their grades.

Another way that neoliberalism has crept into postsecondary education is the lowering of standards. This exhibits itself in two ways. First, since most public universities have been subject to formula funding, the need to recruit more students has become imperative. The formula funding bases the level of funding that the institution receives on the number of full-time equivalent students who were enrolled. In many instances, this resulted in a lowering of admission requirements. In one case, the administration even announced that the score on the ACT required for admission was lowered to 16 while the average score ranged between 20 and 34.

One of the secondary results from this was the increase in the number of remedial classes offered at universities. I argued against this as a misuse of resources. Remediation should be done by community colleges. The other way that standards were lowered is by state governments linking funding to graduation rates. Consequently, many colleges and universities were forced into lowering requirements. Some even put pressure on faculty to be more lenient on grading.

Universities in recent years have incorporated more "accountability" standards as well. This involves requiring faculty to develop rubrics for all their grading. Rubrics are detailed elements that go into the grading process. So, each assignment has very detailed expectations specifically identified. Values are attached to each rubric element. While it may seem like a fair way to grade and make expectations clear, it also confines the professor to following what amounts to a lesson plan. At this level, classes should be more flexible in terms of what is learned. (Grange, 2017) This honed critical thinking skills much more than highly structured lesson plans. This practice also undermines academic freedom. (Hayes, 2019) This is a vital element in developing critical thinking and analytical skills. Considering how quickly technology and cultural changes occur, this undermines the ability to respond and adjust. As a professor, the more time I spent on developing rubrics or detailed syllabi, the less time I had for engaging the material as it applies to current conditions.

An extension of the neoliberal (business) model of university education is that the focus has turned almost entirely to job training. Students select majors and classes based on a career they believe they expect to pursue. Course selection is based on utility for future employment. This is not the proper focus of a university. A university education should encompass a well-rounded preparation of students to be competent contributors to the community, which includes their careers. This means that they should be taking courses that are generally associated with a liberal education.

The term "liberal" should not be confused with a particular political point of view. What is meant here is that every student should be exposed to the humanities and the social sciences. In order to be citizens who are discerning, they need to have some understanding of the principles in democratic society.

As Dorn argues, we can attribute the success of American colleges and universities to their ability to recast their missions and practices toward the public good. At a time when democracy is under threat at home and abroad, it is imperative that educational institutions prepare students to be active, critical, and morally aware citizens. (McClellan, 2019)

Nicholas Maxwell takes this criticism even further by decrying the failure of universities to promote wisdom. He distinguishes this from what he calls knowledge-inquiry.

Knowledge-inquiry is what dominates universities today. It is, I argue, profoundly irrational, in a wholesale, structural way, when judged from the standpoint of helping to promote human welfare. It is this institutional, structural irrationality that is responsible for the failure of knowledge-inquiry to help humanity learn how to solve problems of living so as to promote human welfare. *Knowledge-inquiry betrays reason and, as a result, betrays humanity.*

Wisdom-inquiry is what emerges when knowledge-inquiry is modified just sufficiently to cure it of its gross irrationality. According to wisdom-inquiry, the basic aim of inquiry is wisdom, construed to be the capacity, the active endeavour, and possibly the desire, to realize what is of value in life, for oneself and others. (Maxwell, How Universities Have Betrayed Reason and Humanity--And What's to Be Done About it, 2021)

Maxwell challenges the universities to become more engaged in the community. The separation of these institutions from society has resulted in serious failures to confront today's biggest challenges. (Maxwell, Universities Betray Reason and as a Result Betray Humanity, 2021562*564)

I experienced this firsthand at my first faculty position. I was sharply criticized for a couple of my specific activities. First, the other faculty questioned the value of my research. They interpreted consulting work as just a side hustle. I was expected to do basic research. What I was doing was applied research. I would work with agencies in the public sector (my degrees are in public administration, so this makes sense). In this work, I interviewed all the members of the organizations and examined their policy documents and practices. The results of these interviews and reviews were to draw conclusions about trends in organizational behavior, along with offering recommendations for more effective practices. My colleagues thought that this was not real research. Instead, I should conduct more literature reviews and propose a hypothesis and test it using statistical methods. While there is value in such studies, I placed a higher priority on helping public organizations. I have serious reservations about much of the basic research that is conducted. I will get to this later. The difference that I could not convince the others of was that my field was different from theirs. My field is public administration, and they were all political scientists. These are quite different from one another.

The other criticism was that my community service was to be the faculty advisor for the student government. The associated students were a serious matter in that these elected officers were responsible for a sizable budget and influence on university policies. My colleagues thought this was rather peripheral and that I should be on university committees. I argued that we needed to recognize that many of these students would go on to public office (and many of them did, including legislators, city managers, and even a lieutenant governor). Therefore, it was important for someone like me to be involved with them so that they could learn how to deliberate and abide by the rules of debate, etc. In both instances, what I was doing was closer to Maxwell's wisdom-inquiry. I ultimately left the university as it was clear that I was likely not going to get tenure or promotion.

Building on Maxwell's concerns, the universities tend to elevate themselves above the necessary problem-solving needed in the community. One of the biggest contemporary failures is to convince the public that human-caused global warming is a real threat. Even though nearly 99 percent of scientists agree with this, there are still enough naysayers that policy has not been changed adequately. This is what is called a "wicked problem." It is not easily solved and requires a concerted effort. The current U. S. administration is enacting policies that go in the opposite direction. The question is how it is that so many scientists have declared this emergency, and yet the community is not convinced.

Part of the answer lies in over-specialization. Unfortunately, general practice is that those who go into the sciences tend not to take courses that develop the skills necessary for political persuasion. So, the strategies needed to stimulate political shifts and commitment are not developed by the people who know science. There have been efforts by leaders outside the university who have tried to persuade the public that this is a grave matter, e.g., Al Gore. Ironically, the response to those efforts is that they are not bona fide experts. When scientists put out publications and other communiques, they use technical language and confusing data. This demonstrates the disconnect between the universities and the public. They need to either pair up political scientists or public relations experts with the scientists or they need to teach more of the skills to the scientists themselves.

What has been lacking is both a deep-level dissection of the roots of the crisis and a cross-sector, cross-disciplinary consensus about how we might address it—both in terms of research but also *via* urgent practical change regarding how the institutions are governed, managed, and structured. Moreover, given the complex makeup of academia and its institutions, and the pressing and "wicked" nature of the socio-ecological challenges that threaten long-term wellbeing for all ("sustainability"), solutions need to offer a realistic plan for how prudent, meaningful change might be operationalized at scale and at pace. (Iain S. Stewart, 2022)

All of these factors lead to dysfunctional universities in that there is far too much infighting, isolation, narrowing of discussion, and an improper focus on job training instead of higher education. This naturally contributes to our dysfunctional organizations. If young people come out of our education system, including K-12 and our universities are prepared for a world that no longer exists, they will be hard-pressed to make the kinds of changes to our organizations that are sorely needed. The complaints by employers should be taken very seriously.

Chapter 10:
Postindustrial Organizations

We live in a distinctly different world, especially when it comes to our organizations. It doesn't matter if they are private, public, non-profit, or a non-governmental organization. What we need people to do in organizations is completely different than those in the industrial age. It's about time that we face this reality. We hire very few people to perform repetitive procedures in assembly lines. Most of that is done by technology. More of our organizations are made up of various kinds of problem solvers. Even in the service industry, the expectation is that employees will be problem solvers. Far fewer employees are "cogs in the machine" than in the past. This means that we need to eliminate dehumanizing practices.

This changing organizational environment not only demands that we change the nature of the workplace but also means that we have to change the nature of leadership:

The demands of this new environment will increasingly require organizations to rely on and exploit the knowledge, skills, experience, and creativity of all of their employees – and that will require a new approach to organizational leadership. (Picken, 2012)

Empowerment should replace control as the organization's focus. Control was always an illusion, anyway. Recent studies have shown that increasing individual power pays considerable dividends. In assessing four different empowerment strategies, one study found that a unit increase in granting power to employees has a very large effect on reducing perceived barriers, suggesting to policymakers that granting power to employees is a crucial practice. While providing information is positively associated with perceived barriers, offering rewards and providing access to knowledge and skills are negatively associated with perceived barriers. (Demircioglu, The Effects of Empowerment Practices on Perceived

Barriers to Innovation: Evidence from Public Organizations, 2017) The reason that this is much more important in this century is that we are dealing with more and more "wicked problems." These are highly complex challenges that require multiple points of view to understand and address.

We need to rid ourselves of the notion that the manager is the only one with the knowledge to solve problems. If, for example, the team is made up of 10 people, including the manager, we have the choice of one brain working on the problem or 10. Common sense would dictate that it is far more likely that 10 brains are better than one. The challenge is for both the manager and the rest of the team to accept responsibility for solving problems. We tend to remain locked into the notion that only the manager should develop solutions. The manager should be more of a leader and less of a controller. The rest of the team also needs to recognize that they have an important role. Under the old rational approach, all decisions were to be made by the manager. Sometimes, the manager would consult with the team. What I have seen is that even when this happens, the team is disinclined to take a chance in offering solutions. Empowerment goes both ways. The manager needs to be secure enough to listen to other ideas, and the staff needs to feel confident that they can share different views.

In many instances, we need to take this a step further. It is more common to operate in networks and clusters, with less hierarchy and smaller self-managed work groups. The rigid hierarchical structure of bureaucracy inhibits such practices. Providing the network option is one way to develop a meaningful way to view highly complex and consequential issues. It intersects the various perspectives of various agencies and organizations. The participants gain some additional knowledge and an appreciation for the complexity of the issue at hand. It also mitigates some of the "turf wars" that frequently inhibit problem-solving. (O'Driscoll, 2021) However, it may be necessary to rely more on hybrid arrangements than on choosing one or the other. Eugene Bardach has argued that a combination of networks and hierarchy can be very effective. Using the example of the Incident Command System, he shows how this can work:

The ingenuity of an implementation hybrid begins with ways of taking advantage of sources of productive power at relatively low cost. For instance, it takes advantage of the division of labor into two subsystems, one for resource exchanges and another for coordination of action. Further, it enjoys transactional efficiencies when it manages resource exchange by acting mostly in the network mode, but gains efficiency in managing coordination functions by acting in the hierarchy mode. It realizes still another efficiency by utilizing largely the same personnel to man both subsystems but relying on these personnel playing different roles with one another, depending on which function they are performing. (Bardach, 2017)

Here in Montana, we witness the effectiveness of these hybrid structures with the Incident response teams that deal with our numerous forest fires. There are multiple agencies involved in the process. Communication of expectations and roles is a high priority. This is essential because people's lives and property are at stake.

It is also possible to rely more on a network or cluster within an organization. This is likely more challenging since the hierarchical model is so completely ingrained. The reality is that the manager is not always the person with the most knowledge or passion for a particular problem or issue. This requires a kind of leadership that is willing to let go of control. Rotating the lead role based on the circumstances opens up the possibilities of more appropriate and creative solutions. Sometimes, a more matrix-style of organizing is more effective. This is an arrangement where there is more than one line of influence. So, a person may work in one department but also be officially connected to another. A human resource specialist could be housed in the Department of Transportation but also answer to the policy function of the Department of Administration. Even more to the point, the notion of leadership and communication functioning as a fixed pyramid or spokes does not reflect reality. Interactions and reliance operate in multiple directions. The charts below demonstrate the more accurate relationships.

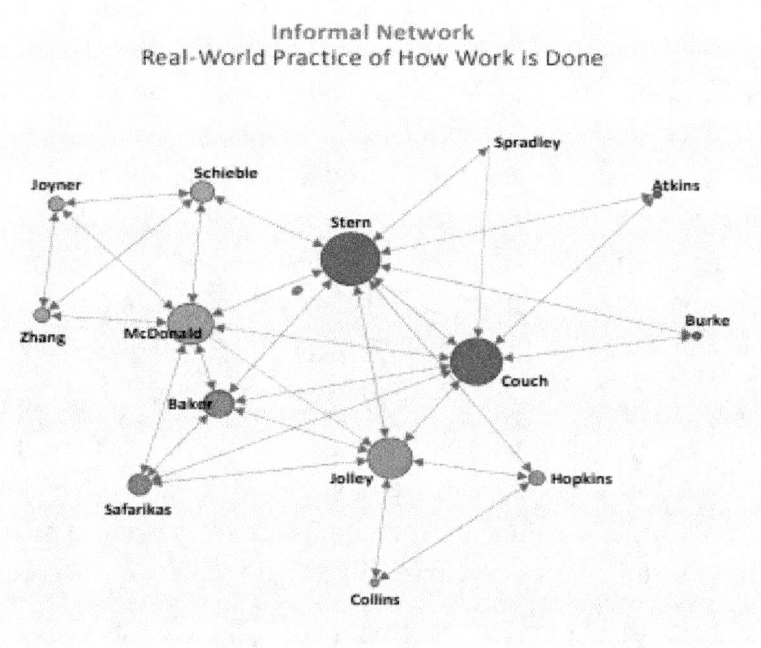

Figure 4: Sample Network (O'Driscoll, 2021)

This demonstrates a simpler network of relationships than one would find in most organizations. When we expand this to include all the relationships that influence processes outside of the organization, the result is an intricate web of overlapping relationships. Insisting on everything being done in and through the straight hierarchy is both unnecessary and undesirable in today's world of work. Hierarchy was created to manage and control information. In the information age, it is impossible to control information. So, it makes much more sense to rely on networks and clusters that may or may not be stationary. When using this form of organizing, it necessitates relationship building. It simply cannot work without it. This stands in opposition to the adage that "we have to work together, but we don't have to be friends." You may not have to be bosom buddies, sharing all your life secrets, but you do have to get to know one another. The more we know about our colleagues' work styles, strengths, personalities, and challenges, the more likely we are to identify how we can work together effectively. Again, we are not rational beings. We are emotional and relational (social) beings.

The key is that innovation and creativity are highly valued. That means we must dispense with the idea that people become positions. Positions are replaced with roles. One person should be expected to carry out multiple tasks instead of overspecialization. This requires very different ways of organizing. One thing this will impact immediately is our concept of leadership. The idea here is that there should be a full range model of leadership that encompasses and distills what is unique about the various styles. In other words, there needs to be various styles exhibited by individual leaders as well as more than one leader. This is readily accomplished by using project teams. While projects usually include a project manager, that does not mean that this person is the leader per se. Rather, this is the person responsible for coordinating the people and processes of the project. It is understandable that we still need an ultimate arbiter. Sometimes, a decision needs to be made when there is no agreement. This is where the hybrid approach comes into play.

The goal of a de-bureaucratized organization is to enhance coordination between groups. It is crucial to get rid of the silos that inhibit interagency cooperation. Silos interfere with creativity on many levels. First, they tend to be rule-driven and rigid in their practices. Consequently, they tend to apply the same solutions to every problem. Secondly, most of the wicked problems we confront today cannot be segmented into separate bureaus. The complexity requires information and skills from multiple sections of the organization. As mentioned in the chapter about bureaucracy, decision-making cannot necessarily be carried out in a bureaucratic manner. Sometimes, the decisions have to come from outside the organization. Using the Cynefin framework, it is easy to see that relying on the industrial model to make decisions is foolhardy. Cross-pollination between units is critical for making tough decisions.

Outcomes are more important than outputs. One feature of the Rational/Industrial model is to measure success by counting output. For example, I was asked to conduct a performance analysis of a public program that provided job training for unemployed clients. The agency reported that a significant number had completed the program and had been placed. However, I decided to measure the number of clients who had (Placeholder1) jobs after 7 months. Part of the program included on-the-job training (OJT). The OJT provided a match for the employers who hired the clients for six months. The result of my analysis was that there was no significant difference between these clients and those who had not taken the job training program. Apparently, the OJT employers tended to discharge the clients when the match stopped. The number of people completing the program was the output. The number of people who were long-term employed was the outcome. In the post-industrial workplace, outcome is going to be vitally important. This is especially the case where there are increasing numbers of people working from home. It is more difficult to measure output for remote workers.

While we are at it, we should get rid of the hourly wage and the 40-hour work week. This practice was applicable to manufacturing, especially if it involved shift work. I have observed way too many employees who have periods of time where it doesn't take 40 hours to complete their tasks, and other times where it takes more than 40 hours. If we compensate people for outcomes, we will be attaching pay to the correct standard. It will likely improve performance because the members of the team will understand that the more they produce or process, the more they get paid. It also gives more flexibility and discretion to team members and is more empowering. This can also go far to improve work-life balance (I actually prefer the idea of "work-life harmony"). Pay for performance is not always appropriate, but it should be used more often than it is. The key is how performance is measured. Evaluations are a key element in most pay-for-performance policies. It is vitally important that evaluations be tied to clear goals that include those outcomes that are under the employee's control. (Ingrid Smithey Fulmer, 2023)

A key concern in any organization, especially those dealing with complex issues, is motivation. In industrial organizations, the common belief was that money was the main motivator. This was more a matter of folklore than any structured study. Frederick Winslow Taylor recommended that higher performers should receive higher pay, but his main focus was on improving efficiency and setting standards. (Taylor, The Principles of Scientific Management, 1911) Subsequent researchers found that money was not necessarily a primary motivator. Abraham Maslow argued that as money served physiological and safety needs, it served as an incentive to work. However, this did not ensure motivation. Rather, it was the higher-order needs of self-esteem and self-actualization that were motivators. (Maslow, A Theory of Human Motivation, 1943) Frederick Herzberg clarified that money, security, and social needs were hygiene factors. That is, they were necessary but did not lead to satisfaction, but their absence could lead to dissatisfaction. The higher-order needs were the motivators. (Herzberg, Work and the nature of man, 1966) Others built on these ideas, including Vroom's expectancy theory, which focused on the employee's expectancy of a given reward for a certain standard of performance. It was not the money itself but the level of confidence that the reward would match the effort. (Van Eerde, 1996) These models are quite helpful in the kind of work associated with industrialism.

When the task is clearly defined, using these concepts of motivation is effective. However, in the tasks associated with post-industrialism, the tasks and solutions are not so clear. As noted by Dan Pink, in cases where even rudimentary cognitive skills are required, these incentives usually don't work. (Pink, 2011). This is where the challenge of leadership and organizational culture comes into play. The motivating factors that really count are autonomy, mastery, and purpose. (Pink, 2011) The important thing here is that the changing nature of work and organizations requires that we focus on those three issues and let go of the notion of management being about control. I will discuss how leadership needs to change to accommodate this in the next chapter.

Another aspect of 21st Century organizations is the need to be nimbler than ever before. Markets, trends, and expectations shift far more rapidly than ever. This is a result of the speed of information transfer facilitated by digital technology. Consequently, organizations don't have the time to go through the hierarchical processes used in the past to make changes. This requires more autonomy at each level. Increased flexibility helps to respond to rapidly changing circumstances. Organizations need to institutionalize and deinstitutionalize far more readily than in the past. They need to institutionalize when procedures are shown to be effective. The use of standardized practices helps to free up creative energies to deal with the more complex problems. This also improves the likelihood that they can be more equitable in the treatment of clients and customers. On the other hand, they also need to deinstitutionalize more quickly as well. This is crucial when systems are not working properly.

As I noted in the description of the Cynefin framework, when organizations remain stuck in the routine or standard procedures, they risk "falling off the cliff" into chaos. It is imperative that members of the organization quickly recognize when something is not working. This is an "all hands" issue. It is not unusual for rank-and-file members to recognize problems earlier than those in management.

In light of all this, the present form of our organizations cannot do this. They may try more open processes, but they inevitably fall back on Rational structures and practices. The dysfunctions that I have already described in some detail point to this reality. If we continue to hold on to Industrial beliefs, we will struggle even further to address the very real challenges of the 21st Century. When I taught the principles of bureaucracy, I pointed out that Max Weber's description of the phenomenon was very logical, elegantly presented, and wrong. The fixation with rationality works until we add people. We may chuckle a bit when considering that people screw up a rational organization. It is because we are not rational beings. We are emotional and relational beings that attempt to use rational principles. We cannot and should not attempt to be Mr. Spock from *Star Trek* fame. It's not that we can't be reasonable. It's more than that, as a collective group, there is so much diversity in our viewpoints that we are unable to navigate the complexity of our challenges through logic alone. We tend to have different "logics" in confronting problems. These should not be ignored by asserting control. We also have different strengths and preferences. In addressing challenges, we have to accept the principle of equifinality, that is, there are multiple ways to get to a solution.

Moving to post-rationalism does not mean that we exclude rational thought. It means that rational thought is only one aspect of the process of problem-solving. Consider again what is presented in the Cynefin framework of decision-making. Three of the four quadrants don't rely exclusively on rational thought. The complicated quadrant includes some rational aspects but also a process of "tweaking" existing processes. This would largely be done by the people applying the process. The complex requires that we incorporate practices that may never have been associated with the task environment involved. The chaos quadrant advocates "winging it."

When I speak of the Rational model, what I mean is a belief in cause-and-effect relationships that are discoverable. Once we have identified the cause to gain a certain effect, we replicate it in standard operating procedures. The other very important part of rationality is that people are objectified. We do not make decisions that take people into account, but positions. That is why it is so common (and maybe easy) for organizations to lay off thousands of workers. There is no thought of how it impacts people. This has gotten worse over the years. That is because we have so objectified people that we now operate in what I like to call "malignant capitalism." The decision makers are so far removed from the people in terms of both customers and workers that they don't even see them. In the 1960s, a trend began that stipulated that all focus should be on the shareholders. This resulted in failures to invest in the workforce and service practices that hardly consider the customer. From their perspective, this is all very rational. It is no wonder that there is little loyalty to the worker and the worker to the organization. In the next chapter, I will consider the 21st Century options.

All of the attributes of dysfunctional organizations prevent the kind of changes necessary for the 21st Century organization. In order to have effective networks, relationship building is essential. When leaders and some employees are arrogant, they fail to draw upon the incredible resources that exist in the organization through its people. When there is no trust, it is impossible to expect leaders or colleagues to let go of control enough for creative problem-solving to occur. When there is a lack of transparency, many of the elements of the wicked problems are not revealed, resulting in poor decision-making. When everything is about control, there is little chance that people who have great ideas and solutions will come forward. It also leads to only a few people taking responsibility for problem-solving.

When managers lack the training necessary to encourage a vibrant, creative team, vital resources in terms of talent and insight are lost. When conflict skills are lacking, the creative process is stymied, and energy is lost because it is devoured by unnecessary conflict. Add to the fact that so many people are miserable in their jobs because of all of the above, they lack the kind of commitment and drive to solve problems or to support one another. Opportunity is lost, and people are dehumanized through all the dysfunctions.

Chapter 11:
21st Century Leadership

The concept of leadership itself must be questioned.

So much is written about leadership that it appears to suggest that all success depends on these wonderfully enlightened people. What if that is not the case? The real question is how much it is about leaders and how much it is about followers? Tolstoy wrestles with this in his book, *War and Peace*:

And therefore, to explain how the submission of millions followed from their relation to one another, that is, how from component forces equal to a given quantity A, there followed a resultant equal to a thousand times A. The historian is inevitably bound to admit that force of power, which he has renounced, accepting it in resultant force, that is, he is obliged to admit an unexplained force that acts on the resultant of those components. And this is just what philosophic historians do. And consequently, they not only contradict the writers of historical memoirs but also contradict themselves. (Tolstoy, 2004)

What Tolstoy wrestles with here is the phenomenon of thousands of men [sic] leaving their homes and their fields to go kill and burn the homes of others they do not know. What caused them to participate in the war between France and Russia? Historians claim that this calamity was brought about by the leaders. However, the vast majority of the men {sic} never knew or heard either the tsar or Napoleon speak. The concern is that too much credit is given to the leaders. He further offers that there can be three possible explanations.

These questions may be answered in three ways: (1) by maintaining that the will of the masses is always unconditionally delegated over to that ruler or those rulers whom they have chosen, and that consequently every rising up of new power, every struggle against the power once delegated, must be regarded as a contravention of the real power.

Or (2) by maintaining that the will of the masses is delegated to the rulers, under certain definite conditions, and by showing that all restrictions on, conflicts with, and even abolition of power are due to non-observance of the rulers of those conditions upon which power is delegated to them.

Or (3) by maintaining that the will of the masses is delegated to the rulers conditionally, but that the conditions are uncertain and undefined, and that the rising up of several authorities, and their conflict and fall, are due only to the more or less complete fulfilment of the rulers of the uncertain conditions upon which the will of the masses is transferred from one set of persons to another.

In these three ways do historians explain the relation of the masses to their rulers. (Tolstoy, 2004)

This is a question for the ages. How do we get to a point where credit is given to leaders in the face of so many followers? Even in organizations, there is, at the very least, consent of the masses to cooperate with the leaders. If it is just an economic transaction, one would think that we would negotiate a better deal. It also points to my question: why are so many people so miserable in their jobs? Part of Tolstoy's answer is not particularly gratifying but may well be close to the truth:

The theory of the transference of the will of the masses to historical characters is only a paraphrase, only a restatement of the question in other words.

What is the case of historical events?

What is Power? Power is the combined will of the masses vested in one person.

On what conditions are the wills of the masses vested in one person? On condition that the person expresses the will of all men [sic]. That is, power is power. That is, power is a word the meaning of which is beyond our comprehension. (Tolstoy, 2004)

Power is something given, not taken. That may seem a little naive. The only way to explain that large numbers of people cooperate with a small number of people is that they give consent. They give consent because they have to have some means of survival. That is, they need a job. It is this leverage that creates power. However, it doesn't necessarily convert to effectiveness or efficiency. As noted in the discussion about motivation, physiological and security needs do not lead to motivation. The intrinsic rewards are more likely to result in sufficient motivation to deliver high quality. Just the same, motivation may not result in effective problem solving, especially if the participants don't collaborate effectively.

I write this because there is too much emphasis on leaders and not on followers. The image we are presented is that the leaders have the answers. Followers either wait for the wisdom of the leaders to be bestowed on them or for the leaders to ask them. This creates a system of communication that is linear, where creativity and discourse are stifled. Many times, we also operate under the impression that there is a "boss." This concept is archaic and contributes to more dysfunction. It conveys the impression that our first responsibility is to comply with the wishes of the one in charge. This is a highly problematic impression. Simon Sinek challenges this well when he says: "It's not about being in charge; it is about taking care of those in your charge." (Sinek, 2025)

Once, when I was interviewing for a job as president of a community college, I was asked about how I would promote the interests of the college. My response was that I would encourage every member of the organization to take on that responsibility as well. Of course, as president, I would have the unique responsibility of advocating and representing the institution. But that would be only part of what is needed. I could tell by the nonverbals that this response fell flat. I wondered about that reaction for some time after that. I came to realize that this is the image we continue to value for our organizations. That led me to reconsider what is truly meant by leadership. I still hold the belief that everyone in the organization is responsible for its success. However, there is a greater need to develop solid relationships for this to happen. To create an organization that can be successful in the 21st century, we need to reset the idea of leadership, especially as it relates to followership.

By viewing leadership and followership as products of adaptations that have emerged in human evolutionary history to facilitate group action, it provides the foundation for more proximal, social-psychological models of leadership. Evolutionary theory accounts for the existence of personality differences in leadership on the basis of traits like ambition, extraversion, and intelligence. It accounts for the relatively stable impressions that followers hold about leadership, such as intelligence, health, and generosity, thus offering the underpinnings for cognitive models of leadership (Lord & Maher, 1991). At the same time, it provides clues as to why these stereotypical impressions might sometimes change, for example, in the presence of an acute intergroup threat (Hogg, 2001). (Vugt, 2006)

Van Vugt presents an interesting take on leadership. Essentially, he asks, "Where does leadership come from? Is it a matter of personal traits or the situation itself?"

My initial response is, "Yes."

Certain traits would come into play under certain circumstances. It connects back to Tolstoy. The leader arises from the expectations of the masses, or in the case of organizations, the employees. Since the nature of the organization has changed in the 21st Century and has changed significantly from the 20th century, it is clear that we need different forms of leadership. The crux of this is that authentic leaders are better for 21st Century organizations. The authentic leader is more likely to improve the performance and development of both high and low performers. (Lucas Monzani P. R., 2014) Ultimately, we must recognize that there is a gap between what we know and what we are doing.

There is a vital need to resolve the leadership gap. That means we have to address leadership vertically and horizontally. If we are going to de-bureaucratize, we can only accomplish it through leadership development both horizontally and vertically. This is one in which everyone fills a leadership role. (Julie A. Chesley, 2020) The current model relies too heavily on the intelligence of the leader in the position. Different circumstances require different strengths and analysis. We also need to acknowledge that there are different forms of intelligence. It is about time that we recognize that everyone can contribute to the problem-solving needs and complexity of the postmodern world. The idea is that there should be a full range model of leadership that encompasses and distills what is unique about the various styles. The truth is that leadership style might be situational. (Sun, 2017) The objective is to replace the term "leadership" as it implies an established position, with "leadership" as it exhibits a level of task-oriented performance. (Coughlin, 2014) More to the point, we need leaders who are more facilitators and seek out the talents and intelligence that result in better decision-making.

This will also require a different form of leadership development. In the industrial age, we primarily have transactional leaders. This means that their role is to set standards, monitor behavior, and dispense rewards or punishments. Now, what we need is a different kind of leader, one who is committed to the growth and development of everyone in the organization.

In summary, we believe leaders can either help followers grow or keep them where they are. Our study shows that in terms of performance criteria, authentic leaders belong to the former group, and transactional leaders belong to the latter. Talent managers should choose which leadership style best fits their organizational needs and act accordingly. (Lucas Monzani P. R., 2014)

This will be difficult to find in our given circumstances. The education system generally does not develop such leaders. It would not make sense to wait until it does. That means that we need to develop them through other means. Joe Raelin argues that there needs to be leadership/professional development *in situ*, i.e., on the job. Professional trainers need to be more internal. There remain particulars that impact leadership practices within the organization. (Raelin, In Leadership, Look to the Practices Not to the Individual, 2020) When people learn leadership exclusively through generic courses, they will tend to standardize practices. Instead, they should learn the overall principles and sufficient critical thinking skills to ascertain what practices need to be applied. Then, once they are within an organization, they work with a coach or mentor to hone the skills they need. The most important point here, though, is that leadership is not something imbued in one person. It is a practice of the entire team:

In the case of leaderful practice, I have registered a commitment to a kind of practice that unabashedly embraces an ideology of democratic participation by all involved actors in forming communities within which members through social critique may have a better chance to resist oppression and other forms of inequitable social arrangements than through reliance on sole heroic leaders (Raelin, 2011) … I embrace enabling structures that support democratic and emancipatory processes that spur the reflexivity of any practice to preserve a sustainable future. (Raelin, Leadership-as-Practice: Antecedent to Leadership Purpose, 2021)

Thus, when I speak of leadership, I intend that to mean something more in line with Raelin. The postmodern organization requires a structure that is much more fluid and draws upon the discourse of all its members. Some may see this as a cumbersome process that involves voting, etc. That is not the intent here. When we use a more collaborative approach, voting is not necessary. In fact, when I work with clients, I clearly state that voting is a bad idea. Voting, by its very nature, is divisive. As people lose votes, they will tend to become alienated. This process is not as chaotic as one may imagine. In most cases, it already takes place. People discuss processes and purposes already. This just elevates those conversations to more formally recognized ones. It also contributes to what Weick calls sensemaking. (Weick, K. E., Sensemaking in Organizations, 1995) In his enactment theory, he describes how the organization responds to ecological change. It doesn't just happen because leadership decides to change. It happens because the people in the organization equally respond to the shifts around them. (Weick, K. E., Sensemaking in Organizations, 1995) The important thing here is to recognize that the evolution of organizations is not just the result of management decisions. Rather, it is the entire body of members and stakeholders who bring about adaptations.

All of this leads us to a starkly different image of leadership. In today's complex organization, we need to discard the concept of heroic or charismatic leadership. The notion of leading must become much more fluid. The entire organization must be able to flex to the constant shifting of the environment. The leader's role is to facilitate that as much as possible.

Industry surveys (PwC, 2017); Deloitte, 2017) and provocative scholarship (Pfeffer, 2015) paint a consistent picture of a shortage of leaders prepared for the (Julie A. Shesley, 2020)disruptive nature of the digital age. To maintain the essential capacity of strategic agility, leaders today must be capable of managing paradoxical tensions, sensing new possibilities and perspectives, and making complex decisions quickly and effectively (Lewis, Andriopoulos, & Smith, 2014). While these capacities have been identified and are agreed upon as important by organizations and scholars, they are difficult to effectively and consistently demonstrate. Currently, less than 10% of leaders have the qualities of mind to optimally lead in volatile, uncertain, complex, and ambiguous (VUCA) environments (Ghemawat, 2012; Leslie, 2009). This shortage of prepared leaders is often referred to as "The Leadership Gap" as a concept that emphasizes the growing difference between the leadership skills currently possessed by leaders in today's organizations, and the skills that are needed to solve the complex problems of the future (Weiss % Molinaro, 2005).

To be clear, we definitely need to learn more about the leadership gap. If, as I suspect, we are to genuinely de-bureaucratize, we can only accomplish it through vertical and horizontal leadership development. Organizations need leaders who don't require ego defense. We need to face the fact that in our organizational experiences, we must be able to deal with a constant state of ambiguity. This is an enormous requirement that we are not currently able to confront. The shift is happening now, and we cannot continue with "business as usual" if we expect to accommodate it.

Without a doubt, the most common request I get for workshops is "communication." Of course, that doesn't really narrow it down much, but it is significant that it is the most common request. People recognize that this is a constant challenge. This is especially the case whenever we talk about leadership. The first law of communication is that we cannot communicate. (Watzlawick, 2011) We are doing it verbally or non-verbally all the time. Is there any stronger message than when someone refuses to talk to us? Yet, we are generally terrible at it. Part of the problem is that most of us are not taught effective communication skills. The most important skill is listening. Before all else, effective active listening is essential for successful relationships. Most of us listen to respond rather than comprehend. As noted in the conflict skills section, this causes most of our problems. This is doubly important in leadership. Yet, it is woefully lacking.

Recent research has given us a list of principles for leadership and communication. I am paraphrasing here from an excellent article. (Gigliotti, 2016)

Leaders cannot <u>not</u> communicate. This bears repeating because so many leaders I have consulted with are unaware of the many messages they send intentionally and unintentionally. This also applies to those who take on situational leadership.

Leadership communication is a process that involves negotiation rather than the transmission of meaning. The truth of the matter is that communication is something that is co-created between the leader and the follower. I go back to the number of times that I worked with leaders who were convinced that they had made expectations clear. It seems as if there is an inverse relationship between a leader being convinced that they are clear and the clarity in the minds of the followers. The confidence gets in the way of clarity. A post-industrial leader needs to be aware of the need for negotiating meaning.

Communication dynamics create a history that shapes and guides future influence efforts. This goes to the heart of developing trust and relationship building. If a leader fails in transparency in a couple of instances, it becomes extremely difficult to create a culture of trust. Leaders should spend time assessing whether or not their communication practices have lent themselves to a healthy workplace environment.

All leadership communication is intercultural. There is no separation between a person's work life and personal life. This is especially the case in terms of communication. Messages are filtered through a person's experiences, regardless of where they occur. Both leaders and followers must be mindful of how these filters work. The evolution of the organizational culture itself also must be taken into account.

Leadership communication always has both content and relational consequences. This stands out as one of the biggest contributors to conflict in the workplace. In almost all my interventions, it is the relational message that has the biggest impact. This is why relationship building is so crucial. If the people in the organization don't do the work of building relationships, it is likely that more offense-taking will happen. This leads to a conflict cycle that is extremely difficult to untangle. This is such a key to 21st Century leadership because the organization needs to rely on the cooperation and creativity of everyone to face increasingly complex issues.

Leadership functions occur in all social decision-making. The important point here is that even the seemingly small decisions matter. I worked in an organization at one point where the monthly team meeting took place at a particular coffee shop. The seating and noise levels were not conducive to a productive meeting. I found myself struggling to maintain a connection with the meeting. The leader had not taken into account how everyone sustained attention. As a person with ADHD, this did not work for me. The manner in which decisions are made should be flexible. There are times when more collaborative decisions are more appropriate.

Leadership opportunities are not something that one waits for; rather, they are situations leaders must create. I take this one with a grain of salt. Since the leader and follower create meaning, it is more accurate to say that sense-making occurs through the two. Through the use of verbal, non-verbal, and para-verbal messages, the team engages in sense-making. To present it as the leader being somewhat exclusively responsible to create opportunity and situations does a disservice to the active engagement of everyone on the team.

There is often a gap between what leaders know and intend, and how they behave and the impact of their actions. This ties directly to the idea that actions speak louder than words. I have witnessed numerous cases where the leader declares that they believe in teamwork. Then, when there is conflict in the group, they do nothing. It is imperative that a tone is set that is consistent with actions. The gap also exists where the leader views themselves as one thing, but others see something completely different. This calls for authentic action.

If leaders want others to be committed to solutions, they need to engage those individuals in naming and framing the problem. This is especially true in organizational change. In the rational approach, the leaders go about defining a problem, developing a solution, and then presenting it to the team. This is completely ineffective. Instead, the followers need to be brought in for the definition of the problem. Frequently, those "in the trenches" understand the nature and details of a problem much more than the leaders. It's the subtle issues that are likely to torpedo new plans.

Initiating the learning process for the group builds stronger leader-follower collaboration than does simply describing the conclusion one has reached through their own learning process. This is the call for the learning organization. One of my favorite adages as a leader is "we can all always get better." Consistently looking for ways to improve not only leads to better results but to healthier organizations. Leaders and followers should be constantly curious.

Listening skills need to be improved dramatically. This applies to leaders and followers alike. This means adopting active listening skills. It is up to each party in a communication transaction to work on clarifying meaning. Just because the other person is nodding as we speak to them doesn't mean they understand. It just means they are hearing the words. The issue many times is people don't want to acknowledge that they don't understand.

These principles, as described in the Ruben and Gigliotti article, point clearly to a more constructivist form of communication. Constructivist communication means that we all understand that we are responsible for establishing meaning. It is not a linear process where information is directed from one person to another. Rather, it is a dynamic system of the intermingling of information. We must remember that we all have different impressions of situations and sense-making due to our diverse experiences. Words and gestures do not have a universal meaning. This is crucial in today's organizations. We need problem solvers, not space takers.

Along with the recognition of the challenges of communication and different experiences, we must consider the role played by different personalities and strengths. This ties closely with the need for leaders and followers to be both self-aware and other-aware. There are so many programs and workshops on personality traits that it has become a regular cottage industry. While I prefer to use the Myers-Briggs Type Indicator® (MBTI), the alternatives can provide the perspectives needed. The most important thing to consider is that people realize the role played by personality. For example, introverts and extroverts communicate very differently. The introvert prefers to process internally and have time to respond. The extrovert, on the other hand, processes externally and sometimes just brainstorms. When a team member misunderstands this and assumes the opposite expectation, there are serious communication failures. Without going through all the dimensions of personality, it should go without saying that misunderstanding another person's preferences can lead to serious disruption and conflict.

Another tool I have used in working with organizations is the Kolbe Index®. This clever tool measures people's natural problem-solving strengths. Since we need more problem solvers in the workplace, it makes sense to understand how we do this differently. I, personally, have confronted this challenge in my work. In my case, I tend to be a simplifier, adapter, and innovator. These traits tend to be the opposite of those of most people who work in my field. Consequently, I have been accused of being careless or uncooperative. I acknowledge that my collection of strengths points to being non-compliant. However, this is actually my strength. I will approach problems from a perspective of identifying different solutions than the routine or standard processes would yield. I also acknowledge that I rely on people on my team to counterbalance those strengths. I need people who are planners and stabilizers. When the people on my team recognized this, and I recognized their value in the differences, we developed into an excellent team.

If organizations are going to take advantage of the differences we find in one another, both followers and leaders need to take notice of those differences. The challenge lies in how to apply this knowledge in today's work environment. This is where more flexibility comes into play. Industrial organizations relied on standardization and people doing the same thing. This results in people doing the same thing over and over for years. As a result, life is sucked right out of them. There is no reason that human beings should be crammed into such practices. In the post-industrial organization, we should take advantage of diversity and develop ways to vary jobs with cross-training and innovation. When we create a project team, we should intentionally incorporate the different strengths. It would make no sense to do otherwise. We can apply the same practice to the ongoing operations as well. Leaders have the responsibility to empower employees to grow and develop. This may be accomplished by applying the knowledge gained from various assessments to help both high and low performers. (Lucas Mnzani, 2014) High performers don't need to be "pigeon-holed" because they are effective at what they do. Remaining static only undermines a vibrant team. I am convinced that the vast majority of low performers are a matter of bad fit. No reasonable person would take on a job to intentionally suck at it.

The key to successful teams, especially in terms of problem-solving, is empowerment. This applies to leaders and followers alike. This relates back to autonomy, mastery, and purpose when I discussed motivation. The use of these three values is all empowering. If employees and leaders are empowered, they are more likely to come up with creative solutions to difficult issues. A comprehensive study of governments that have used empowering strategies showed "that the most effective method for reducing perceived barriers to innovation is granting power to front-line employees. (Demircioglu, The Effects of Empowerment Practices on Percieved Barriers to Innovation: Evidence from Public Organizations, 2017). Empowerment must be authentic and not just a device to get more cooperation out of followers. I have witnessed many occasions where management has announced empowerment opportunities that only go through the motions. This is a matter of genuine trust. Sometimes, mistakes will happen, and the team members must be allowed to learn from them. I will come back to this in the next chapter.

One sure sign of empowerment, or the lack thereof, is organizational silence. This is a phenomenon where nobody raises an alarm when something is wrong. This happened with the Enron scandal and the Volkswagen calamity. The people in the ranks of Volkswagen knew that there was a rigged measurement of pollutants in their vehicles. However, nobody spoke up. This was caught later on by government officials and resulted in serious losses for Volkswagen. In my experience in various organizations, both public and private, I have witnessed instances where people know something was wrong but would not speak up. There is a genuine fear of repercussions if they do. It doesn't matter if this is true or not. What matters is the perception that people will be punished. This is incredibly disempowering. In order for today's organizations to flourish and solve complex problems, everyone needs to feel free to speak the truth.

The Volkswagen case illustrated that the cost of organizational silence can add up to several billion dollars. However, focusing on executives, engineers, or even line workers seems insufficient to reduce employees' silence. In this work, we propose and show some initial evidence that you may need "two to tango", that is, managers with a positive leadership style, but also employees who truly identify with their organization. (Lucas Monzani S. B., 2016)

In this age of information abundance, the most important attributes for leadership are positivity and transparency. Since we really can't keep many secrets, it makes sense to be open and honest. I recall working with a group of upper management leaders who didn't answer questions about new procedures and expectations. When I asked them why, they said they didn't know the answer. "Then, tell them that," I responded. People understand you are human and will allow you grace if you are honest with them. There are many studies that show that positivity contributes to more effective organizations. This is not sappy sentimentalism. It is realistic in the sense that people respond well to positive attitudes.

With followers, leaders need to be very transparent and, in addition, be confident in themselves, hopeful of the future, with both the desire to succeed and a plan to accomplish that success, optimistic toward the future, and demonstrate their resilience to bounce back and beyond. Followers who perceive their leaders to be transparent and positive seem to trust them and judge them to be effective in leading them through challenging times. (Steven M. Normnan, 2010)

We must rely on each other to be successful. These are challenging times in so many ways. The only way we will develop solutions is by cooperating with each other. The way we organize must move from the rigid, cold, top-down structure and behaviors to those that are much more humanistic. In the end, it is all about relationships. It is clear that we need significant changes in how we organize in the 21st century. We need organizations that are nimble, creative, and energetic problem-solvers. Some of the more concrete reforms are the following:

Get rid of the 40-hour work week. It is only necessary for shift work, and that is not the majority of what we do now. There are too many instances where people are just putting in time and accomplishing very little. If they need to work 50 hours, then that is what they will do, but if they only need 30, that is what they will do. A caution here is not to let this be a form of exploitation. One of the worst trends recently is salaried workers putting in extraordinarily long hours. We still need to address work-life harmony.

Stop hiring people for restricted positions. This rigid style of hiring results in periods of intense effort and little to no effort. If people are hired as part of a team and learn multiple functions, they can be more flexible and participate in the work that needs to be done. This also contributes to team member development. This addresses the need for mastery.

Measure performance based on outcomes, not output or process. This also addresses the need to focus on purpose. If people are not focused on the reason for what they are doing, i.e., outcomes, they are more likely to be motivated.

Use more project-centered problem-solving strategies. This should not be associated with the "gig economy," where people don't have a solid attachment to the organization, but should be a normal practice for the permanent staff. It also helps to address the need for autonomy.

Chapter 12: Authenticity

There are literally thousands of books written about organizational leadership. The first thing we need to do is to dismiss and embrace them all. The person(s) who take on a leadership role must continuously search and upgrade their practices. There really isn't one formula for leadership. Rather, there are many resources and opportunities for developing effective leadership. The ideas (theories) include transactional, charismatic, ethical, servant-leader, and relational. These each have some valuable insights, but doesn't always fit either the situation or the individual. They are also very different from the organizational theories of the 20th century. These ran through a collection of macro theories that were applied to all organizations. The initial Classical (Scientific Management) promoted ideas that people are essentially part of a machine. These ideas have not gone away in many respects. Leadership still relies on money as a motivator and views people as objects.

Later theories built on the classical model but still rely on the Rational Model. The human relations approach suggested there are set ways to manage social expectations. Human resources theory advocates structured ways to manage personal and institutional growth through strategic planning and goal setting. Systems theory suggests that everything in organizations can be viewed in terms of input→process (throughput)→ output with a feedback loop. This included people and materials. Deming's Total Quality Management incorporated processes for constantly improving quality for everything and everyone.

All of these theories rely on the application of the rational model of cause and effect. The main idea is to identify the cause and adjust it to achieve the desired effect. On the surface, they present an attractive way of considering management. The difficulty here is that there are innumerable variables that impact outcomes. We are still dealing with people and, like it or not, people are unique individuals. Consequently, the application of any of these universal approaches is unlikely to work. The idea of management itself is a problem. It suggests that the objective of leadership is control. To put it bluntly, especially when it comes to organizations, control is an illusion. This is what leads to the dysfunctions I have already identified. There are a few mentions of followership, and that is a huge problem. Here, I take a considerable departure from mainstream literature. We should consider the practices of everyone in the organization and not spend so much time on so-called leadership. What follows are concepts that apply to everyone. As noted earlier, the nature of organizations going forward is far more fluid than we have practiced to this point.

To move away from the rational model requires a very different mindset. I propose that we consider a leadership triangle. I use the image of a triangle to indicate that the elements are neither sequential nor hierarchical. Rather, they each inform and support one another. The elements of the triangle are Authenticity, Positive Psychology, and Mindfulness.

These are usually presented independently, but really should be viewed as symbiotic. They rely on each other to be successful. Each element supports the other. This interrelated triangle influences the entire organization. It contributes to continual growth for everyone. Unlike other ideas of leadership, this is not a formula for every leader to follow. Instead, it calls for a constant striving for growth. In many ways, it is associated with Aristotle's concept of virtue ethics. In virtue ethics, there are no codes or rules; there are no justifications for behavior as in consequentialism; and there are no identified ideals as in teleological ethics. The leader, and everyone else for that matter, constantly strives to be virtuous. This involves keen self-awareness and a commitment to life-long learning. I will unpack each element of the triangle and, in the process, show how they interact with each other.

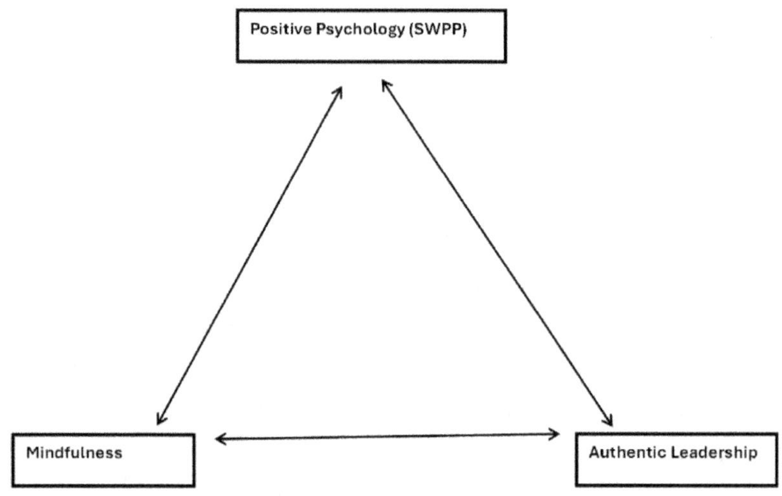

Figure 2: Post-rational Model

A more recent development has moved away from the more standardized versions of leadership to the idea of authentic leadership. Notice in the brief description that certain terms are not used, such as employees or managers. This is quite intentional, as the focus is away from standard language that implies hierarchy and does not turn people into objects. The four elements of authentic leadership are **self-awareness** and **self-regulation**. **authentic action**, and **authentic relationships**. From this point, I will refer to authenticity instead of authentic leadership. Authenticity applies to everyone. (Puck M. Altera, 20132) The sooner we move in this direction, the sooner we can overcome the dysfunctions.

The source of authenticity is tied to positive psychology. A branch of psychology that focuses on strengths and behaviors that build a life of meaning and purpose. This is not based just on fleeting happiness but on the pleasant life, the good life, and the meaningful life. Authentic leadership is also informed and supported by practicing mindfulness. Mindfulness is essentially living in the present and being fully aware. I will address authenticity in this chapter and positive psychology and mindfulness in the next two chapters.

The authentic person is confident, hopeful, optimistic, resilient, transparent, moral/ethical, future-oriented, and gives priority to developing associates to be leaders. The authentic leader is true to him/herself and the exhibited behavior positively transforms or develops associates into leaders themselves. The authentic leader does not try to coerce or even rationally persuade associates, but rather the leader's authentic values, beliefs, and behaviors serve to model the development of associates. (Avolio, 2003)

Self-awareness – This truly is the linchpin of authenticity. It invokes the opposite of both Dunning-Kruger and impostor syndrome. Authenticity requires that we recognize both our strengths and weaknesses. This is not an easy task either. I have known many people over the years who genuinely do not know themselves. One might say that this can be a lifelong journey. It is also not static. One needs to learn to adapt to changing circumstances. We need to let go of the notion that anyone, including the leader, knows the whole team's jobs or is an expert in everything. Only a fool would believe that they have knowledge beyond everyone else. The authentic person takes the time to recognize his/her abilities and preferences. There are many assessment tools available to help with this process.

The process of self-awareness involves being open to what Richard Rohr calls the "true self", as opposed to the "false self" (Rohr, 2011). The false self is the one that identifies itself with its possessions, reputation, status, or accomplishments. The true self is the one that identifies itself with its relationships, virtues, identity, emotions, motives, and goals. (William L. Gardner B. A., 2005) The true self recognizes that we are all connected, along with being unique. It completely rejects the notion that any of us are "self-made."

I have been asked in workshops if it is possible that a person's authentic self is a jerk. My short answer is no. The jerk is typically extremely insecure in themselves. They are fearful that someone will discover their vulnerabilities. So, by being a jerk, they keep people away from knowing their insecurities. The rough exterior is just that, an exterior. The interior is frightened and confused. They will do everything they can to keep that hidden. On several occasions, in my work as a consultant, I have come across these folks. As soon as I start to get close to seeing the real person, they turn on me. I am usually hired by them to fix everyone else. I don't particularly like getting dumped as a consultant, but that becomes necessary if they continue to put up the barrier. On one occasion, I ended up telling the manager that I was unable to help them because he was unwilling to cooperate. I recognized that he was the problem. Of course, he made it sound like he had fired me. I followed the biblical advice and shook the dust off my sandals and moved on.

There are many tools around to assist in the process of developing self-awareness. Personality assessments can be very helpful, but not all are equal. Some of them overlap with behavioral habits. The difference can be extremely important. Personality traits are generally our preferences or tendencies. They influence behavior, but they don't determine it. They may even shift a bit over the years, but typically not a lot. Behavioral habits, on the other hand, are the kinds of things we adapt over the years either as a defense mechanism or to accommodate others. An example of a behavioral habit is what is often called being a "people pleaser."

The personality assessments I prefer are the Myers-Briggs Type Indicator (MBTI)® and the Enneagram. The MBTI uses four pairings – extrovert/introvert; sensor/intuitive; thinker/feeler; and judger/perceiver. (Myers, Introduction to Type: A Guide to

Understanding Your Results on the MBTI Instrument, 1993) It is important to work with someone who is certified in MBTI to use this device because there can be some significant misunderstandings. The key is that the subject must be comfortable with what the assessment says about them for it to be helpful. The Enneagram is a personality system that focuses on emotions and how they drive our lives, as well as how we engage with others. It identifies nine personality types, each possessing its own strengths and weaknesses. (The Enneagram Institute, 2026) This is a very useful tool in understanding how we relate to people around us.

Again, it is wise to work with someone who is certified in the Enneagram to avoid misuse. It is important to note that these are assessments and not tests. When responding to the questions in each of these, we need to go with what comes to us first. If we treat it as a test, we are trying to get the correct or most desirable response. Another useful assessment is the Kolbe A Index®. This assessment measures our natural strengths. These are particularly important when we are striving or problem-solving. In the 21st century organization, this is extremely important. The Index is divided into four modes: factfinder, follow-through. Quick start, and implementer. This assessment is particularly useful in the workplace. It helps to identify who has the appropriate strengths for specific tasks. It also helps anyone recognize areas in which they don't have the appropriate strength. When working against strength, we experience conative stress. This is a common problem in many workplaces. People are expected to perform in all areas, even though that may not work to their strengths.

Another benefit of the assessments is that they also help us to recognize the differences in others. This is perhaps the greatest obstacle to highly functional organizations. People in the organization get frustrated with how others behave, especially when it comes to how they organize and solve problems. Knowing that this is a matter of natural preferences and strengths goes a long way toward better cooperation. Having this knowledge can reduce the instances of offense taking, as well. When we understand that people are acting a certain way because of who they are, we are less likely to assume they are doing it to annoy us. Sometimes, self-awareness is just as much a matter of knowing more about us as it is recognizing how others are different from us.

Another key issue in self-awareness is understanding our own values. It is truly surprising to find out how little we know about our values. Often, we assume that we have certain values because the culture dictates that to be the case. However, this is frequently not the case. It is also important to recognize that our values can shift over time. One assessment I find useful in measuring our values is the Portrait Values Questionnaire (PVQ). (Schwartz SH, 2001) The instrument uses a series of statements in which the respondent decides whether or not it describes themselves. The result is a hierarchy of values that the individual possesses. Knowing more about our values can help us to consider whether we are honoring them or not. It also gives us an opportunity to reflect on the fact that we should revise our values. For the most part, it is an effective tool for improving our ability to be authentic. The question being: "Am I true to my values?" Of course, if my values are self-centered or shallow, there is a different process that must take place. If, in this case, we are honest with ourselves, we need to take steps to correct counterproductive values. It will likely take some form of intervention to make this happen. The outcome of the self-awareness process is to develop both better leaders and followers (these being roles and not necessarily confined to particular persons).

Self-regulation – having achieved a level of self-awareness, individuals need to engage in the ongoing process of self-regulation. This is a matter of paying attention to how my behaviors are impacting those around me. Self-regulation is an ongoing process. It is vital that a person be a lifelong learner. In some ways, the term itself is a bit misleading. It implies that this is done entirely as an individual. That is not the case. Rather, self-regulation requires a considerable amount of social interaction. (Mortimer, 2025) For example, if someone is considering taking a direction that they have never experienced, it is helpful to engage with those who have had that experience. A key part of this in the organizational environment is seeking and properly processing feedback. We learn from our peers, authority figures, and those who report to us. This is a matter of learning from both positive and negative (or constructive, if you wish) feedback. This tool empowers anyone to reflect on what happens next after receiving feedback.

Self-regulation is the human capacity to control urges or temptations to develop more constructive behaviors. It is generally intentional and requires a certain amount of discipline. (Soniya Billore, 2023) In Bandura's social cognitive theory, this involves three elements: personal factors, behavioral factors, and environmental factors. (Jesus de la Fuente, 2022) The personal factors include the cognitive (everything we learn), the affective (emotions, values, personality), and the conative (skills, strengths). The behavioral includes things like coping strategies, responses to policies, and ways in which we seek help. The environment includes organizational culture, work-life balance, and learning experiences. The process involved follows a general pattern. We think of something that is possible, an idea, a plan, a change, or any strategy. This is called forethought. We then set out to carry out the new behavior. Then we reflect on how well it went and how it might be revised. This process repeats itself. This is the essential process of self-regulation. Done properly, we should become better people in terms of performance and interactions.

For leaders and followers alike, the process of self-reflection is crucial. We learn from each other in so many ways. When we pay attention to our impact on others around us, we learn what works. This is a critical part of being an organization. Over the years, I have learned much more from peers, supervisors, and reports. This does not mean that I change myself in order to belong. It means that I learn more about myself through reflection on those around me. I discern what kind of person I am and want to be by observing others and listening to their feedback. (Qingqing Li, 2023)

The key to self-regulation is that it should be rooted in positive attributes. This is because the root of authenticity in organizations (as well as other parts of our lives) is centered in positive psychology. I will discuss this further in the next chapter. Suffice it to say, the person who is self-aware and chooses to self-regulate should be one who wants to advance their virtues. This process of reflection is also rooted in mindfulness. This is the discipline of reflecting in a disciplined and constructive manner. I will expand on this in Chapter 14.

Authentic action – The third principle in authenticity is to convert the virtues attained in self-regulation to action. This is an area of some debate. In the tradition of authenticity, mostly found within existentialist philosophy, the viewpoint is that people make choices about their purpose in life and who they want to be. (Catherine A. Helmuth, 2024)

Extending this philosophy into the principles of authenticity associated with organizations, Kernis listed the four areas as awareness, unbiased processing, relational authenticity, and action. (Kernis, 2006) The key authors of the authentic leadership concept have a slightly different list. Walumbwa et al describe the principles as: awareness, balanced processing, relational transparency, and internalized moral perspective. (Walumbwa, 2008) While I understand the need to focus on how one internalizes their moral perspective, how this converts to action is far more important. (William Gardner, 2005) One can internalize a principle of not lying, but it doesn't mean anything unless they don't lie. I have certainly witnessed many leaders and followers alike who claim certain moral principles, but they really don't show up in their actions. I can't say whether they truly believe what they claim, but I can observe whether or not it converts to action. My experience with the church bears this out more than any other I have had. Many of the people that I interacted with were sincere in their beliefs (or at least they forcefully claimed so). However, their actions were not consistent with these beliefs. I witnessed more back-stabbing, lying, and inconsideration than I ever expected. I was very disappointed with the experience. Don't get me wrong. I met plenty of good people in my church experience. However, the position in the church seemed to have an inverse relationship with virtuous behavior. Actions do, in fact, speak louder than words.

The key to authentic action is the relationship between authentic leadership as related to leader behavioral integrity, which in turn is associated with follower affective organizational commitment. "Being authentic refers to an open and non-defensive way of interacting with one's environment. As a result, leaders who function authentically express their person-self, yet at the same time, remain open to relational input." (Hannes, 2012) While most of the literature emphasizes this as leadership advice, this applies equally to everyone in the organization. In fact, it is reasonable to expect that, on occasion, those identified as followers are the ones to take the lead in authenticity. It is everyone's responsibility to empower ethical behavior. A leader's integrity is essential to the team's commitment to the organization's success. This is accomplished through both attitude and action. Follower perceptions of authentic leadership predict employee job satisfaction. There is also an interaction effect of leader self-perceptions and follower perceptions of authentic leadership in predicting job satisfaction. There is an integration between the leader and follower perspectives. (Matej Cerne, 2014) It is extremely important to acknowledge that this requires a certain amount of authenticity with all members of the organization. If one who is labeled as a follower is not authentic in their self-awareness, self-regulation, and action, it is unlikely that they will respond to the authentic action of the leaders. What I have seen is that the absence of authenticity prevents the achievement of the same in others.

Authentic relationships—The expectation is that through increased self-awareness, self-regulation, and authentic action, authentic relationships will develop. It's really not that simple. It is not a linear progression. Instead, the three processes include relational development along the way. We become self-aware both through reflection and interaction with others. The key is to pay attention to the reactions of others. That doesn't mean we take responsibility for their reactions, but to be open to learning something about ourselves from the experience. This is especially the case when we have repeated patterns of responses from others. If the pattern is positive, it is imperative that we figure out why that is the case. What is it that I did or said that resulted in that response? If the pattern is negative, we might consider alternatives. The key here is that we need to recognize these experiences as indicating something about ourselves.

I had an encounter with an individual who was frustrated in her job. She complained that she was repeatedly getting into conflicts with others. I asked her the obvious question: "What do you see as the common denominator here?"

She thought about it for a while and realized that it was probably something she was doing. I encouraged her to keep thinking about it to figure out what was common in the pattern. It took a few days, but she came back to me and admitted that she was expecting to be affirmed when she asserted a point of view. Instead, she was getting challenged. This was largely a matter of personality differences. When I reviewed the personality results for the team, I discovered that she was the opposite of most of her colleagues. Consequently, she was looking for the response that she needed as an extrovert-feeler, and her colleagues were introvert—thinkers. When the extrovert voices ideas, she is just processing and not looking for answers. This is especially the case with a feeler. They look for answers that relate to how it impacts people, and the thinkers were offering logical responses. In our follow-up discussion, I helped her formulate a better way to process her ideas. It was important that she not project particular expectations on the others. However, she also needed to explain her needs when it came to brainstorming ideas. Months later, I met with the team, and it was clear that the team's vision had improved considerably.

When addressing self-regulation, we don't just do it internally. We require feedback from others. This means that we recognize things in ourselves that we may be suppressing that interfere with building positive relationships. (Donna Ladkin, 2016) We accomplish what Jung called "individuation" through reflection on our own actions and the feedback we get from those around us. (Donna Ladkin, 2016) There are some concerns that this may also involve two selves. The self that regulates and the self that needs to be regulated. This is really just oneself as we continually learn and, hopefully, grow. It is in the ongoing process of relationship building that all of this takes place. We certainly need to make a decision that we want to improve relationships at work. This goes right to the heart of correcting one of the main dysfunctions in organizations.

Authentic action is how we accomplish building authentic relationships. After all, we aren't mind readers. We learn about each other through our actions as well as our words. Since communication is constant, this process takes place whether we are authentic or not. The challenge is to be willing to pay attention to our actions and those of others. Being authentic also requires that we do all that we can to avoid offense-taking. When we recognize that we are responsible for our behaviors and our interpretations, we are well on our way to authentic relationships. It is equally important that we recognize our shadow side as well. There are attributes that we all have, some we suppress, that still define who we are. I can say, as a personal example, that one of my shadow sides is that I am a "people pleaser." That may not sound like such a bad thing, but it can lead to some rather negative behaviors, and it can be inauthentic. I have caught myself trying to please others by doing things like overcommitting or compromising my own values. The important thing is to recognize these things and do our best to correct them.

Authenticity is a key element to improving how we organize. Complete authenticity is not possible, but moving toward it is. It is certainly a good way to improve our relationship-building. The challenge is to allow ourselves to be who we are at the same time that we are progressing. We can all always get better. Authenticity does not stand on its own, however. We need other tools to complement it. We need to understand and apply positive psychology to build on strengths and manage weaknesses. We also need to practice mindfulness in order to engage in self-awareness and self-regulation without judgment. The next two chapters explore these two concepts more thoroughly. (Patricia Duarte, 2021)

Chapter 13:
Positive Psychology

In 2000, Martin Seligman, the new president of the American Psychological Association, urged his colleagues to consider a different focus in psychology. (Seligman. Martin E. and Csikszentmihalyi, 2000) Their concern was that, up to that point, the field had focused on disorders and dysfunction. Instead, they promoted the idea of also focusing on human strengths, human potential, and excellence. Seligman and Csikszentmihalyi argue that there is a compelling need for this other side of psychology.

At this juncture, the social and behavioral sciences can play an enormously important role. They can articulate a vision of the good life that is empirically sound while being understandable and attractive. They can show what actions lead to well-being, to positive individuals, and to thriving communities. Psychology should be able to help document what kinds of families result in children who flourish, what work settings support the greatest satisfaction among workers, what policies result in the strongest civic engagement, and how people's lives can be most worth living. (Seligman. Martin E. and Csikszentmihalyi, 2000)

The ideas behind positive psychology relate to prevention more than to treatment. It calls upon psychologists (and other social sciences) to focus on human attributes that overcome challenges. It also fostered an increase in research and advocacy for happiness studies. Other aspects include a better understanding of attributes like optimism, courage, future-mindedness, interpersonal skills, faith, work ethic, hope, honesty, perseverance, and the capacity for flow and insight. (Seligman. Martin E. and Csikszentmihalyi, 2000)

In terms of organizations, the argument is that positive psychology will improve performance. For example, Shawn Achor argues that happiness fuels success, not the other way around. (Achor, 2010)

The idea is that when we are positive, our brains function better. Much of the positive psychology literature is rooted in the science of happiness. What has been found is that people seek happiness in the wrong places. The first fallacy is the phenomenon of "mis-wanting." This is where we believe we will be happier when we get certain things or achieve objectives. However, most times when we attain these, we do not feel either a great sense of joy or a long-lasting one. There are a variety of reasons for this. It may be a matter of hedonic adaptation; over time, the thing we're so excited about loses its luster. For example, when we get that new car, it is exciting for a while, but it doesn't take long for that excitement to wear off. The problem may also be a matter of "impact bias." This is when we overemphasize the impact of an event. We either mispredict the intensity of the event or we mispredict the duration. Sometimes, it is a matter of fiscalism – we tend to focus on one thing, forgetting everything else. Consequently, we may neglect many of the things that are really important. This is something that happens when we are so narrowly focused on achieving a goal that we neglect our family or other close relationships. One of the things that is really common in our culture is our tendency to engage in relativism. We are comparing ourselves and our possessions to those around us. This may cause us to not appreciate what we do have and only stress what we don't have.

The happiness literature offers us alternatives to "re-wire" our brains to counter all of the things that miss the mark. The following are suggestions on how to increase our happiness:

Exercise – when we exercise regularly, we feel better physically, of course. But we also feel better psychologically. It reminds us that we do have more control over our bodies and directs us to recognize how much we can accomplish. I have kept an exercise routine for almost 40 years now. There have been plenty of times when I had to convince myself to go to the gym. I can say this; however, I have never regretted it.

Using your strengths – We all have unique strengths. As noted in the authenticity material, we are better off discovering what they are and finding ways to apply them. Sometimes, we may have to do things that go against the grain of our strengths. When that happens, we should offset that by either mixing in tasks that do use our strengths or discover way of accomplishing the same outcome with the strengths we do have.

Gratitude – This is the big one. Being grateful empowers us to recognize the good things in our lives. I am convinced that the biggest shortage we have in our culture is gratitude. We are so caught up in what's "wrong" or missing in our lives that we fail to see all that is good. One way to combat this is to regularly take time out (preferably at the beginning of the day) to list three things we are grateful for over an extended period. This tends to help rewire our brains to think more positively. Many times, it's the simplest things that we lose sight of in terms of what we should appreciate. (Hallward, 2010)

Social Connection – This goes directly to one of the key attributes of dysfunctional organizations. We are social beings. When we don't foster healthy relationships, it interferes with our ability to be happy. It is crucial that we do the work necessary to have good relationships. When I have worked in groups where this does not happen, I find myself not liking my job and somewhat grumpy when I get home. On the other hand, when I do have strong relationships at work, the job is less stressful, more rewarding, and generally more productive. I can think of a couple of times, especially where I had positive relationships. When I was in the Navy, it was generally the case that the people I was stationed with took care of one another and spent the time getting to know each other. In my last job, I worked with a great team, so much so that we still get together and support each other. When I worked with people who criticized each other, remained distant, and complained a lot, I was not happy, even though I might have loved the actual work.

Meditation – This is one that most of us shy away from a bit. Sometimes, we make it more complicated than it really is. The idea here is to learn how to pause and pay attention. I will get into more details in the next chapter on Mindfulness. Suffice it to say that learning how to be present is worthwhile.

Kindness – It is so interesting how doing acts of kindness for others goes so far in contributing to our own happiness. This is because we are truly social beings, and when we act on this, it strengthens our own subjective well-being. This goes right to the heart of the relationship building that is so essential for organizations to be their best. If we strive to be kind and helpful to our coworkers, we are more likely to contribute to both our happiness and the well-being of others.

Using these actions consistently is very likely to move our organizations to better health, creativity, and productivity.

There have been some important challenges to positive psychology that bear some consideration. One criticism is that the ideas are rather culture-specific. The concern here is that not every culture, whether it be a matter of demographics or the organization's culture, will respond positively to the suggestions for improving wellbeing. Sometimes, adjustments need to be made that are more appropriate for the team. However, I would be cautious about dismissing these strategies too quickly. Another criticism is that positive psychology might be too isolated from other fields that are relevant. The issue here is that when changes are made in any social environment, they have an impact in dynamics that are connected. For example, if a team chooses to work on using strengths more appropriately, it could alter some business practices negatively. To avoid this may just be a matter of careful reflection on the interrelationships of the social environment. Probably the biggest concern is that positive psychology relies too much on what is called "individuation." This is a vital part of recognizing the difference between having an organization that is insular or collaborative. Under the present circumstances in our culture, this really is a huge concern. Bauman notes how this results in behavior similar to consumerist practices.

If the human bond is, like all other consumer objects, not something to be worked out through protracted effort and occasional sacrifice, but something which one expects to bring satisfaction right away, something that one rejects if it does not do that and keeps and uses only as long as (and no longer than) it continues to gratify – then there is not much point in trying hard and harder still, let alone in suffering discomfort and unease in order to save the partnership. (Bauman, The Individualized Society, 2001) This would certainly suggest that if the focus is just on our own happiness, it is likely to fail in the long run.

One might think that these criticisms torpedo the whole idea of positive psychology, but such is not the case. As with many of our ideas, the critiques are the seed for the maturation of the idea. In this case, the challenges have resulted in what is called "second wave positive psychology" (SWPP), which recognizes that overall well-being and flourishing require a healthy approach to positive and negative aspects. Bad things do happen. It is a matter of how we deal with them that becomes important. (Lomas, 2016) SWPP is based on four principles: appraisal, covalence, complementarity, and evolution. Appraisal focuses on the importance of not identifying phenomena as either positive or negative. For example, it is unwise to label emotions as either positive or negative. We may experience anger and still have it be positive, particularly when it is a matter of righteous indignation for an injustice. Even concepts like happiness and sadness can be viewed either way. Excessive or superficial forms of happiness, usually those associated with hedonistic pleasures, can lead to poor decisions. Extreme levels of happiness, either too high or too low, can easily lead to unfortunate consequences. By applying the principle of appraisal, a balance can be achieved. In the next chapter, we will see how using mindfulness will contribute to better appraisal.

The second principle of SWPP is covalence. This principle involves a recognition that many of the desirable characteristics advocated by positive psychology possess a light and a dark side. The best example is our common experiences of love. This brings us both the hope and anticipation of love returned and the fear of rejection. When we love, we do enter into an area of risk. Co-valence reminds us to hold these contradictions in balance. This ties into the appreciation of embracing ambiguity that I mentioned as associated with authenticity. It is also worth noting that there are a variety of forms of love. The most common is noted in the Greek term, *filios*. This is the general kind of love we experience with our friends and community. When we are open to such closeness, we also risk being hurt. Then there is the passionate form of love or *eros*. This is the romantic love that most of our love songs are about. An essential challenge in this type of love is that it is associated with high levels of passion, with all its idealizing of the other. It is entangled with our natural sexual needs. The darker side of this is that sometimes it clouds our judgment. The third variant of love is *agape*, the ultimate level of selflessness that exists at a virtuous level. Whenever we embrace this high level of humanitarianism, we open ourselves to abuse, even to the risk of our lives or well-being. As Bauman noted so well: "to love means opening up to that most sublime of all human conditions, one in which fear blends with joy into an alloy that no longer allows its ingredients to separate." (Bauman, Liquid Love: On the Frailty of Human Bonds, 2013)

This brings us to the third principle, or dialectic, complementarity. This entails a recognition that the two competing dimensions inherent in the positive characteristics, especially love, are not aberrations but are the essence of them. This idea is rooted in some of the Eastern philosophies. (Lomas, 2016) It entails the recognition that change and growth happen through the interaction of positive and negative. While the negative is not particularly desirable, it plays a role in developing wisdom and resilience. An organizational team might experience a setback that was not anticipated. This could be a shift in the market or a development of new technology. Both of these events are rather common today. If they address it by understanding complementarity, they take the time to learn about alternatives and may develop innovative responses. The innovation would not have happened unless the negative event had occurred. Public organizations frequently experience pushback from citizens. If they take the time and effort to listen to the concerns and come up with responses that address the issues, they change both the problem and the tenor of the relationship with the citizens. If organizations and the people within them only see problems as something to avoid, they will not innovate. If, however, they recognize that every problem is an opportunity, they will grow and achieve more than they would have otherwise. (Denhardt, 2011)

Finally, the principle of evolution sets the overall context for SWPP. The overall premise is the belief that people and organizations evolve. The central tenet is that, in the long run, this evolution will lead to better circumstances. Even when an organization dissolves, it can be viewed as a positive outcome. For one thing, it may be a matter that the mission of the organization was completed. This has been one of my own experiences. I was selected as the president of an international church reform organization. When I assumed the role, the organization had several projects underway. We were publishing a newsletter and providing consulting services for communities around the world. Over the course of the years in my tenure, we had fewer and fewer members. At first, this was a depressing turn of events. After a while, we came to recognize that we had served our purpose and our publications would remain in circulation, which would continue to help communities with information they needed to thrive. We no longer needed to meet as a board and voted to dissolve the association. Looking back, I have learned that this was a good thing because it allowed all of us to move on and engage in other social justice activities. I grew considerably during this experience, but it was time to move on. The essential nature of SWPP that differs from the first wave positive psychology is that it takes on a dialectic profile rather than a positivist one. The difference is a recognition of the interacting roles of positive and negative aspects of our lives. This fits well with my advocacy for moving past the Rational paradigm, which is itself positivist. Positivism is simply the belief that cause-and-effect relationships can be known. The problem with it is that most of the events in our lives involve many variables and no single cause.

Applying the features of positive psychology (which, from this point, will refer to the second wave type) leads to the proposals associated with Positive Organizational Behavior. Subsequent to the publications about positive psychology, many scholars focused their attention on what was called Positive Organizational Scholarship. This is defined as "a movement in organizational science that focuses on the dynamics leading to exceptional individual and organizational performance, such as developing human strength, producing resilience and restoration, and fostering vitality." (Cameron, 2004) In other words, this developing area of study emphasizes the attributes that make organizations successful that are associated with individual and group traits. Out of this, evolved concepts of Positive Organizational Behavior, which focuses more on the positive behaviors themselves. (Fred Luthans and Carolyn M.Youssef-Morgan, 2017) Luthans defines Positive Organizational Behavior as "the study and application of positively oriented human resources strengths and psychological capacities that can be measured, developed, and effectively managed for performance improvement in today's workplace." (Luthans, 2002) The four elements of positive organizational behavior are hope, self-efficacy, resilience, and optimism. (Fred Luthans and Carolyn M.Youssef-Morgan, 2017) These are central to leadership and performance in 21st Century organizations. They apply to team members as well as leaders.

Hope is defined as motivation that is generally positive. It requires that the individual or team be confident that they can achieve a goal. Goal setting is the main behavior associated with hope. Many organizations go through planning exercises that involve establishing goals. Unfortunately, most that I have observed only do this to "check a box." Lengthy meetings are spent developing goal statements that are typically complex. Considerable effort is spent on wordsmithing. When I work with groups, I usually have to explain what a goal is, since what I see most of the time are mere platitudes. I point out that a goal statement should be such that we can answer the question, "How do we know when we have gotten there?" For hope to be genuine, the individual or group must have the agency (authority to do it) and a fairly clear idea of how they will accomplish it. The other issue that frequently interferes with hope is that the group identifies too many goals. Ordinarily, what I find are plans with 10-15 goals. The general rule of thumb is that teams should set 3-5 annual goals. (FranklinCovey, 2025) When they set 11-15 goals, they typically accomplish none of them. Hope cannot be dispersed so thinly.

Self-efficacy is a matter of believing that the individual or group has the ability to mobilize the motivation and the resources to accomplish the goal. This is tied to Albert Bandura's social cognitive theory. Bandura asserts that people can alter their behaviors to achieve more positive outcomes through guided reinforcement. "Four approaches are recognized for efficacy development: mastery or success experiences, vicarious learning or modeling from relevant others, social persuasion and positive feedback, and physiological and psychological arousal." (Bandura, 1997). This is distinct from hope in that it is evident in the actual carrying out of the goal. This is something I have seen get in the way of achievement all too often. The team sets a goal or goals, and that is pretty much the last they hear of it. On so many occasions, I ask a manager or team member about their plan, and they have to look for it. It does not impact their day-to-day activities much at all. For planning to be effective at all, the team must focus on their accomplishment and alter their behaviors accordingly. This is also an area where I consider relationship building to be absolutely crucial. Adjusting behaviors will involve knowing who has the relevant knowledge, skills, or abilities. It also requires considerable trust in colleagues and transparency in leaders. As I have already noted, these are not common traits in organizations.

Resilience is the ability to navigate challenges, setbacks, or even failures. To be truly resilient, the person or teams have to expect that they can not only get through the tough spots but come out of them even better than before. The adversities can include conflict, which is an area of considerable weakness for most teams. Since few people are taught how to engage in healthy conflict, this ends up devouring huge amounts of energy. It hinders resilience because the typical conflicts tend to become cyclical, with mutually reinforcing behaviors. The Arbinger Institute refers to these as "collusions." (The Arbinger Institute, 2018) Teams that have resilience deploy positive adaptive patterns and processes to overcome adversity. A recent example of resilience was the response to the Covid pandemic. Organizations needed to respond to very dramatic impacts virtually overnight. The adjustment to massive shifts to remote work was an extreme challenge. For my own team, we had to switch from in-class training to virtual in a matter of a couple of weeks. We developed online material at a furious pace. We proved resilient by meeting this challenge, even increasing our participation levels. The delivery of classes became quite innovative overnight. This was the case all over the world. It did change the world of work profoundly. Unfortunately, many organizations are reversing this trend by insisting that workers return to their offices. Even though the level of performance had not suffered any setbacks, the need for control prevailed over the gains in morale and outcome-based practices.

Optimism is a matter of how we explain things. It attributes positive events to things like personal effort, permanent gains, or pervasive causes. At the same time, it explains negative events as temporary or situation-specific causes. It is a general expectation that in the end, all will be well. This is not a matter of looking at the world through rose-colored glasses. Instead, optimists expect that success can be achieved and that growth will occur. They expect good things to happen. (Seligman, 1998) This has been presented by consultants and authors over and over. As much as this is the case, what I have found is just the opposite. Organizations that I have consulted for and those in which I have worked tend to have a much more negative view. People describe themselves as powerless and that nothing will ever change. I see this as a broad state of affairs. In current events, especially political and economic, the mood is one of despair paired with anger. It is very difficult to encourage people to be more optimistic in the current environment. If there is one area in which I have experienced the most pushback, it would be here.

Positive Organizational Scholarship and Positive Organizational Behavior are very similar to one another. They are both evidence-based, relate to the workplace, and rely on scientific exploration. POS is more of an academic exercise, and POB is more of an applied area. Frequently, I hear people aver that things like POS are "just theoretical." This needs to be addressed here. There is relevance to scholarship, and it does rest in "real life." The scholars who develop organizational theories don't just make stuff up. It is drawn from observation of actual organizations. The scholarship side may focus more on what is called basic research, that is, developing theory itself. The behavioral side concentrates more on applied research, literally entering the organizations. The two rely on each other to achieve a better understanding. In this case, scholars have used extensive quantitative and qualitative analysis to gain a better understanding of what is possible. It could be improved by better interaction between the universities and the public and private sectors, as I noted earlier. Just the same, the scholarship is relevant.

The application of the concepts associated with Positive Organizational Behavior is in what is called Psychological Capital.

Luthans, Youssef et al (2007, p.3) defined psychological capital as one's positive psychological state of development that is characterized by (1) having confidence (self-efficacy) to take on and put in the necessary effort to succeed at challenging tasks; (2) making a positive expectation (optimism) about succeeding now and into the future; (3) persevering toward goals and, when necessary, redirecting paths to goals (hope) in order to succeed; and (4) when beset by problems and adversity, sustaining and bouncing back and even beyond (resilience) to attain success. (Fred O. Walumbwa, 2011)

It is easy to see how this is an application of Positive Organizational Behavior. The key here is that this should become the norm for the organization. In most of the literature I found, the emphasis was placed on starting with the leader. The suggestion is that if the leader displayed these positive behaviors, the rest of the team members would follow. (Suzanne J. Peterson, 2008) I am not so sure that is always the case. Sometimes, a better place to start is with the team itself. There are many occasions I have observed where the team goes through a training about positive behaviors and returns to the workplace, and the leaders are impressed by what they see and take on similar behaviors. It is important for leaders to make behavioral changes at some point, though. If they do not, it will be difficult for the momentum to be sustained. (William L. Gardner B. J., 2005) This is tied back to the authentic leadership model that emphasizes the initiating role of the leader.

Positive modeling is viewed as the primary means by which leaders develop authentic followers. Posited outcomes of authentic leader-follower relationships include heightened levels of follower trust in the leader, engagement, workplace well-being, and veritable, sustainable performance. (William L. Gardner B. J., 2005)

It really works both ways, though. This is an example of how the Rational model influences how we look at organizations. It assumes that those assigned a leadership role are the ones who must initiate behavioral change. It is really a matter of "both/and" when it comes to whether it is about the leader or the followers. In any event, whoever takes on the leadership role toward more positive psychology needs to be convinced that it is effective, or they will abandon it at the first occasion of something not working as planned. (Sean T. Hannah, 2012)

The organization must nourish and recommit to psychological capital on a regular basis. This is not a one-and-done strategy. It requires continuous learning and reinforcement. One of the factors that will indicate that psychological capital is working is whether there is improved subjective well-being. This is a state where the individual has a sense of being in a positive circumstance. It includes the idea of work-life balance (although I prefer the term work-life harmony) (Vincent Cassar, 2013). Well-being is understood in two theoretical levels. The first regards the top-down, or what is called the dispositional, approach. This includes things like personality, motivations, emotions, and cognitive abilities. The second is bottom-up, which emphasizes situational issues like economics and other life circumstances. Interestingly, objective life circumstances have only been shown to influence around 10% of happiness. However, predispositions account for around 50% of well-being. This leaves around 40% that is tied to intentional positivity or that which is more under our control (Fred Luthans, 2013). This may be broken out into relationship and health, psychological capital. Relationship Psychological Capital is defined as "drawing from one's psychological resources of hope, efficacy, resiliency, and optimism in making positive appraisals of relationships and probability for relationship success based on motivated effort and perseverance." (Fred Luthans, 2013) In terms of my discussion here, this is a huge consideration. If people are convinced that they don't have to be friends, it suggests that their Relationship Psychological Capital is not in good shape at all. Health Psychological Capital is defined as "drawing from one's psychological resources of hope, efficacy, resiliency, and optimism in making positive appraisals of health-related circumstances and probability for health-related success based on motivated effort and perseverance." (Fred Luthans, 2013) Health capital involves how the members of the team are taking care of themselves. Complications related to stress are particularly concerning. These complications are discussed further in the next chapter on mindfulness.

The final consideration with respect to positive psychology is the ethical dimension. In this case, virtue ethics is preferred. Virtue ethics is most notably associated with Aristotle. This version of ethics focuses on good lives, rather than basing proper behavior on codes or laws. Aristotle describes virtues as the way one fulfills one's potential. For humans, these virtues include temperance, courage, justice, wisdom, communicative and social virtues, virtues of friendship, prudence, and honor. These are attributes that we develop throughout our lives. Aristotle's virtue ethics faded from view for many centuries, largely because they did not fit with the ideas of law and authority. Ethical values were tied to codes in what is called deontology. The problem is that this tended to encourage a form of minimalism. The questions related to ethics were more those that tickled at the boundaries. The concerns became more about what one could do to stay within the codes. More to the point, what one could get away with and less about achieving any ideals.

The other dominant ethical forms included consequentialism and human rights.

Consequentialism leaves open the question of what is truly measured in terms of the desirable end. For example, much of what we see now is claims made under neoliberalism that the ultimate value or endpoint is the profit margin. It leaves us in a position where much is justified as an "ends justify the means" mentality. The reliance on rights as an indicator of ethics leads to not only a multiplication of rights but also justification for poor behavior in the name of rights. There are so many rights being identified that tend to overwhelm the more basic ones, such as the right to life, liberty, and justice. The use of rights also establishes a situation that places an obligation on others. (Boersema, 2011) The philosophy of rights is naturally combative. It easily becomes a matter of conflicting rights. The biggest problem of ethics based on codes, consequences, or rights is that they assume the source of ethics comes from outside the person. (Zagzebski, 2023) Virtue ethics, on the other hand, places the responsibility for ethical growth and action within the individual. It is crucial that one understands that this is an ongoing process.

This doesn't mean that the individual is free to create virtues that do not contribute to the greater good; quite the contrary. The virtues are those that lead to the good life and the fulfillment of human purpose. There are those that are easily viewed as common ground: compassion, generosity, tolerance, trustworthiness, honesty, sympathy, open-mindedness, intellectual courage, perseverance, carefulness, and autonomy are a great starting point. (Zagzebski, 2023) Understanding what those are and how to activate them is the job of the authentic person. This form of ethics fits quite naturally with positive psychology (SWPP) and certainly with Positive Organizational Behavior. It is the duty of every person, especially those who take on a leadership role, to seek to become more virtuous. One way to embark on this process is to identify people whom we consider virtuous and how they exemplify the virtues.

Given the expectations mentioned earlier that a leader must be professionally as well as ethically competent, virtue ethics provides a way for a leader to grow ethically, much like she grows professionally. For example, finding an exemplary to imitate ethically is much like finding a mentor to imitate professionally, and working to develop a habit of virtue is much like working to develop a habit of a good leadership trait. So, the development of virtues fits well with the development of leadership skills. (Lonnie Gentry, 2020)

Ethics is not a side hustle. It is incorporated into everything we do. I recall when there was a call for more ethical development in academia. After the Enron scandal, the alarm was sent out that we needed more ethical training. Most of the institutions chose to meet this challenge by adding courses in ethics. The alternative was to include ethics discussions in every class. My preference was to do both.

Positive Organizational Behavior, which includes hope, efficacy, resilience, and optimism, goes quite naturally with the promotion of authenticity. To be authentic is to be human, and to be human is to be virtuous. These are two of the three cornerstones to moving beyond the Rational paradigm. This won't necessarily come either naturally or easily. Just the same, they are vital to the flourishing of our organizations and the people within them. A tool that will make this possible is mindfulness.

Chapter 14: Mindfulness

The third side of the authenticity triangle is mindfulness. This has gained considerable popularity in recent years. (Kathleen M. Sutcliffe, 2016) This is a practice that improves the ability to deal with stress and increases self-awareness. Mindfulness is a way of paying attention: on purpose, in the present moment, non-judgmentally, as if your life depended on it. It may also be defined as a state of consciousness. The primary focus is to pay attention to the present moment. What is interesting is how much time and energy we spend ruminating about the past and worrying about the future. In the process, we squeeze the present right out of our consciousness. The process of mindfulness entails paying attention to what is happening in the moment. The focus is on sensory messages, body sensations, and what is happening around us.

Without a doubt, there is plenty of stress in the workplace. Most of the sources of stress are the attributes of dysfunction that I have already described. When there is no relationship building, people become uneasy and unsure of whom they can trust. This also contributes to gossip and complaining about colleagues. These are stressful because most of the people in the organization begin to wonder if they are the next topic. Arrogance instills stress in everyone in the organization. It is a challenge working with such people. For one thing, it is nearly impossible to have a constructive conversation with people who already know everything. Lack of trust in the organization makes everyone feel insecure and wary of those around them. The emphasis on control is stressful for both those subjected to it and those wielding it. People naturally push back whenever they are being controlled. The many untrained managers are causes of considerable stress. The employees are frustrated with the inconsistencies and incompetence of the leaders.

The untrained managers struggle mightily with trying to figure out how things should work. The biggest source of stress is poor conflict skills. Bear in mind that the two most frequent reasons for people leaving their jobs are managers and colleagues. This is a matter of the stress caused by those two sources.

One solution to this widespread stress is to teach mindfulness techniques. To understand this, we need to explore what happens to the mind and body during stress. There are two primary tracks within our bodies when we experience stress. The first is the Sympathetic-adrenal-medullary (SAM) axis. This is sometimes referred to as the fast reaction. The SAM process activates corticosteroids and the peripheral sympathetic nerves. SAM initiates a surge in the secretion of norepinephrine and epinephrine from the adrenal medulla, as well as elevated secretion from sympathetic nerves and locus coeruleus. This generally causes the immune system to degrade, and the reduction in new neuron creation. The process also leads to an increase in blood pressure, while the brain shuts down non-essential neural circuits. Interestingly enough, during such events, one does not think clearly since the problem-solving part of the brain is not fully functioning. This is not always a bad thing. It empowers us to react quickly when danger arises or when we have to perform at a higher level. It also tells us that we should not engage in problem-solving in complex situations while we are stressed.

The bigger problem is the other axis or the slower response, which is mediated by the Hypothalamus-pituitary-adrenocortical (HAP) system. This is the longer-term response, especially to sustained stress. This results in a decreased learning capacity, feelings of anxiety, nervousness, and low moods. The person under long-term stress perceives things people say or do as threatening and negative. This is the phenomenon of self-deception that Warner warns us about. Without any correction or intervention, this leads to more stress and, over time, is incredibly harmful to our bodies. Stress at work can lead to a number of manifestations. These include fatigue, muscular tension, headaches, sleeping difficulties, irritability, and inability to concentrate. One key point is that much of the stress is the result of perceptions of threat or danger.

Mindfulness has been shown to be an effective intervention for perceived stress events, especially those that are long-term. (Anisha Rajan, 2026) Mindfulness-based interventions (MBIs) are believed to reduce stress by activating the parasympathetic nervous system, improving emotional regulation, and enhancing psychologically flexible responses.

Mindfulness, however, facilitates metacognition that goes beyond merely thinking about primary thoughts and emotions, instead altering the very way people relate to them (Teasdale, 1999; Teper, Segal, Inzlicht, 2013). People who can engage in mindful metacognition are able to *detach* and *disidentify* from their thoughts and emotions (Virgo & Silbersweig, 2021) and *reperceive* them as subjective phenomena of the mind rather than objective features of reality (Shapiro, Carlson, Astin, & Freedman, 2006) [italics in the original].

There are varying degrees of intervention from long-term courses to clinical treatment. Even some very short-term practices may be helpful. Learning mindfulness techniques regularly (i.e., on-the-spot), especially when difficult situations arise, may be useful to restore focus and be present to the actual situation. (Hafenbreck, 2017) For more significant events, mindfulness can be very effective at self-regulation in terms of how they respond to perceived crises. This is accomplished through a process of decoupling the self from experiences, events and mental processes that are considered adverse. It is important to remember how much stress is tied to the perception of the severity of these experiences. MBI techniques lead an individual to create distance between themselves and their self-worth and their thoughts, emotions, and experiences. This process has also been described as "decentering," in which a person views thoughts as events in the mind rather than being reflections of reality or an accurate self-view. It is extremely important to recognize how stress, especially long-term, has an impact on subjective well-being and productivity. Research has shown that compared to the pre-intervention period, the intervention period was associated with greater reductions in burnout and perceived stress, improvements in mindfulness, well-being, and increases in team and organizational climate and personal performance.

Probably the most common source of stress in the workplace has to do with conflict. As I have already noted, this is very common. People generally do not know how to handle conflict because they were never taught. I have witnessed this myself very often. So many of my interviews included many tears. Mindfulness has shown itself to be very helpful in dealing with conflict. The first reason should be obvious. When people engage in mindfulness techniques in reflecting on their conflicts, they discover that there are usually many misperceptions involved. This doesn't mean there are no real causes of conflict. Conflict is a natural occurrence whenever people interact with each other. The challenge is to engage in it in a healthy manner. For long-term conflicts, the preferred strategy is collaboration, through which the parties can develop "win-win" solutions. This is nearly impossible if they are basing their understanding of the conflict on perceptions, especially those that result from self-deception. Unfortunately, since people are not very good at conflict, the most popular strategy is to avoid it. This generally results in even greater problems. For one thing, it is common for people in conflict to recruit allies. Mindfulness techniques have been used to improve conflict skills quite effectively. Mindfulness cultivates approaches, attitudes, and behaviors that are more constructive. A key aspect of this is that it changes behavior. For quite some time, it was believed that conflict styles were a matter of personality or disposition, which are resistant to change. However, recent research has shown that behavioral change is not only possible but likely using mindfulness techniques. Further, these techniques led to behavior change that included constructive conflict methods that reduced the use of avoidance strategies. This is especially crucial for those in a leadership role. In my work, I found that avoiding conflict is the most common approach used by managers and supervisors. This is understandable, though. They usually view it as a matter of taking sides. The truth is, there are no sides per se. Rather, there are differing perceptions and understandings of a situation. When applying mindfulness techniques, it becomes a bit easier to work through these differences since the focus is on the present, untainted by deceptions.

Perhaps the most important contribution of mindfulness in enabling authenticity is the importance of self-awareness. This goes well beyond the idea of just being self-centered. In fact, it is just the opposite. It is described as reducing a distorted or biased sense of self and one's relationship to others. This is enacted through a combination of practices that create a meta-awareness of self (self-awareness), and ability to effectively manage or alter one's responses and impulses (self-regulation), and the development of a positive relationship between the self and others that transcends self-focused needs and increases prosocial characteristics (self-transcendence). This supports the notion that the authentic self, if mediated with the mindful self, will be one that is sensitive to the needs of others and continuously reflects on how the self relates to those around them. If a person, especially in a leadership role, embraces mindfulness wholeheartedly, they are more likely to develop compassion. This will be revealed through distinct affective (empathy, indifference), cognitive (common humanity, recognizing suffering), and motivational (willingness to act) aspects of compassion. Applying mindfulness techniques leads to an authenticity that does not include being a jerk. This is an essential step to enacting the authenticity triangle. It also moves us closer to "re-humanizing" our organizations and past Rational objectiveness. This also encourages anyone in a leadership role to pause when considering situations, a vital step in developing better solutions. This same self-awareness contributes to the ongoing development of virtue.

Adopting mindfulness techniques goes a long way to accommodating relationship-building. Once the leaders and team members become more proficient at these practices, they can encounter others in a less defensive position. When one can consider a situation from a mindful perspective, they are able to counteract the tendency toward offense-taking. It is much easier to grow healthy relationships if it begins with an acceptance of oneself and others non-judgmentally. We are also able to more readily accept the quirks in others when we consider them mindfully. We are better equipped to relate to others if we avoid the positivity associated with self-esteem. This may sound counterintuitive, but the emphasis on self-esteem has negative impacts on our ability to relate to others. If we base our assumptions on our being "good people," we open ourselves to the possibility of judging others.

Mindfulness also contributes to the development of Psychological Capital. If one can view the present as it is and not fall victim to despair, it is much easier to be hopeful. The idea of setting goals and believing they are possible is much easier when one avoids the habit of focusing on the negative. This is a bigger challenge than most of the people I have encountered seem to believe. Over the years, working with organizations and teaching about goal setting, I noticed that most people were not hopeful. Mindfulness goes a long way to correct that. The Mindful Self is much better equipped to accept self-efficacy as well. A person needs to believe that they can accomplish things first. Then they are more likely to embark on a challenge and follow it through. The mindful person is much more likely to be resilient. When we face challenges or setbacks, we have to be able to pause and consider the situation, removing fears and distortions. Studies have found that continuing mindfulness-based practices improved the overall resilience of teams and contributed to psychological well-being. Trait mindfulness, which refers to a person's general level of mindfulness across situations and time, reduces levels of anxiety. This, in turn, promotes a general positive attitude about the future. Mindfulness is a means to evaluate objectives and situations and be realistic in building Second Wave Positive Psychology.

It is easy to see how mindfulness can go far to overcome the dysfunctions in organizations. Members of the organization draw the wrong conclusions from misperceptions and miscommunication. When individuals and teams take on mindfulness practices, most of these problems are avoided. Many times, it is just a matter of engaging the pause that allows a team to recognize that things are not as they seem. The mindful individual is much less likely to engage in self-deception, including offense-taking. This, in turn, facilitates authenticity in leaders and followers alike. The mindful person is one who is willing to work on continuous self-awareness and virtuous growth. It is also a crucial element in taking advantage of Second Wave Positive Psychology, leading to Positive Organizational Behavior. All of this connects back to building Psychological Capital.

Clearly, there are great ideas in combatting dysfunction in organizations. People do not have to be miserable in their jobs. The question is, why aren't we going there? Or if we do try these things, why do we tend to backslide? The answer is in the need for us to finally surrender our anchoring to the Industrial-Rational model and to move on to what is next.

Chapter 15:
Escaping the Iron Cage

Max Weber, in his *Essays in Sociology*, warned us about the "Iron Cage of Rationality." In his essays, he describes in detail the attributes of a Rational society. This is clearly laid out in his description of bureaucracy. It goes further than that, though. This paradigm took over every aspect of our lives. People were reduced to employees, customers, students, and executives. In terms of organizations, it is clear that the focus is on dehumanizing. The main idea behind rationalism is summed up in Frederick Taylor's *Scientific Management*. He contended that there is "one best way" to do things, and it is discoverable. This is a way to curb human creativity through empirical methods. In order to function, every effort must be made to limit human passion. Working people are alienated from their own labor. This has come to a climax in neoliberalism, where everything is about money. All aspects of life are commodified. This is the idea, anyway. The biggest problem with this is that it is unsustainable. Like it or not, we are still humans with our passions, our creativity, and our virtues. Rationalism has run its course.

The question remains, "How do we respond?" It is likely not one thing or direction. Rather, it will be in multiple ways when it comes to organizations and society at large. The first challenge is learning how to be comfortable with ambiguity. If there is one consistent theme in Rationality, it is the desire for certainty. The belief has been that if we just identify the cause, we can deal with the effect. When it comes to social issues, especially, there are always multiple variables. More to the point, usually, when we treat one cause, it has an impact on others. This is where the Cynefin framework is so helpful. This opens the door to much more creativity than we usually allow. Many of our challenges fall into the complex or chaos categories. They require a very different kind of thinking and problem-solving. This calls upon organizations to resist only going to standard procedures to solve problems. Sometimes, the need to achieve something close to certainty causes unnecessary delays in making decisions at all. If we are more willing to go with approximations or even ambiguity, we will make choices that are timelier.

One huge challenge here is that we still have to work against the education system that remains in the Rational paradigm. Students come out of this system prepared to follow rules and expect simple answers. They have been taught that there is a right answer. I have watched this unfold in organizations many times. The younger employees' first instinct is to await clear instructions. At the same time, they are not prepared to ask questions or to think creatively. A factor that stands out even more is the lack of relational skills. For the most part, collaboration is discouraged. Assignments are individual. In too many cases, collaboration is viewed as cheating. As already noted, employers are complaining about the lack of communication and social skills among new college graduates. Many organizations find it necessary to provide their own training for these areas. This issue is aggravated by the lack of discernment ability relative to evaluating information as credible. Our education system needs a reset. This should be designed more to teach critical thinking and creativity, and not be one-size-fits-all.

The biggest challenge is in relationship building. Leaders and those who take on leadership roles must learn relational leadership. Since we are working more and more with problem solvers, there is a greater need to get to know our teams. We need to consider the whole person, not just their knowledge, skills, and abilities. Very often, people are called upon to work on projects. Consequently, they must be able to form healthy, constructive relationships more easily. This means that everyone must develop the ability to collaborate. When an organization is more insular, this doesn't work well. Members of the team are too focused on their own needs, growth, and success. Organizations become more insular and less collaborative. People tend to identify who is in and who is out. They lack conflict skills, so time is wasted and relationships suffer. Collaborative teams, on the other hand, behave differently. It is normal for people to help one another. It is okay to both ask for help and to give it. These organizations place a high premium on diversity. I don't mean just demographic, but diversity of personalities and strengths. They also engage in healthy conflict. Because they can take time to reflect on interactions and build trust, they counteract offense-taking. Leaders in these organizations are coaches and not managers.

Relational leadership is closely tied to authenticity. People in these organizations seek to improve themselves and those around them. Communication tends to be more effective. This is not to suggest that it is perfect. Perfect communication is not possible, and we need to be okay with that. Communication is considerably more than a leadership tool or strategy. Rather, it is an orientation, a world view, a way of understanding leadership that focuses more broadly on the process of social influence itself. "For those who aspire to lead others, the communication-centered ideas of attention and agenda-setting, the management of meaning/framing, and sensemaking-/sense giving fit well within a systems view of communication." Authentic leaders must reach all levels of the organization. They must identify the strengths of their followers and help them with their development and integration towards a common goal, purpose, vision, and identity of the organization. The elements of authentic leadership, along with the authenticity of all members, all contribute to this. The need for strong relationships is not just a "feel-good" proposition.

Positive interactions in the workplace have been shown to improve job satisfaction and positively influence turnover, as employees who experience support from colleagues are more likely to remain in an organization long term.

Relational leadership, as an extension of authenticity, calls all of us to accept this as our purpose. To counteract what has become a common insular organizational culture, we should explicitly encourage relationship building. Naturally, this begins with our own authentic relationships. We need to focus on everyone's success. This is particularly true for those in formal leadership roles. Most importantly, we need to be present. Pay attention to what is happening around us and apply mindfulness techniques to get there. In paying attention, respect the differences and resist labeling those who think differently as "troublemakers." It is important to deal with conflict promptly, with some exceptions.

The exceptions have to do with time-sensitive issues. That is, if it isn't important in an hour, let it go. All members of the team, but especially those in formal leadership, need to develop "confident humility." This is a consistent willingness to learn from others. Remaining constantly curious opens up many opportunities that would otherwise go unnoticed.

The key to Relational Leadership is a reminder that "it's not all about you." This is a lesson we can all learn from time to time. My first lesson in that was in basic training for the Navy. I will continue to learn it to this day. In paying attention to those around me, I need to focus on learning their interests, skill sets (even those that seem to have nothing to do with our jobs), and strengths. Now for the tough part (for me, anyway) – we need to allow others to help us succeed. Asking for help is a huge challenge in our culture. I know it is for me. We especially need to identify and encourage individuals and groups whose knowledge, experience, skills, and strengths are complementary to our own. Everyone should be encouraged to do this as well. We have to possess the courage to recognize and share our own shortcomings. This is not a matter of false humility but of honesty. Frequently, being honest with us is the vital first step. This is another place where mindfulness will play a role. We must allow team members to shift from "Do this task" to the more empowering, "I need your help." This will go a long way to encouraging others to be helpful.

Relational/Authentic Leadership is a significant departure from Rational thought. According to Mary Uhl-Bien, there are two threads of leadership theory: entity and relational. The entity thread is the primary Rational one. It focuses on the cognitive/affective function of the individual. This cognitive part is how relationships are processed. The relational thread emphasizes relationships as the driving force of leadership/followership…

…it differs in that it adds a perspective of leadership as an outcome. …i.e., leadership is generated in social dynamics – rather than leadership as a formal (managerial) role that drives organizational processes. …[offers] a general definition of relational leadership as a social influence process through which emergent coordination (i.e., evolving social order) and change (i.e., new values, attitudes, approaches, behaviors, ideologies, etc.) are constructed and produced

A significant feature of this way of considering organizational leadership is that it dispenses with the notion of control. The idea that management (managers) exert control over the organization is an illusion. If the members of the organization nudge things in a different direction, that is the more likely outcome. Besides, in my observations, whenever managers try to exert control, especially overtly, the tendency is for the team to push back. Humans very naturally resist control, unless they choose to do otherwise.

To take it a step further, it needs to be recognized that the development of theory, especially in the social sciences, often runs into paradox, i.e., tensions and contradictions. Even in this text, we run into such seemingly contradictory ideas. On the one hand, I argue for more open processes to bring about more authentic leadership. On the other hand, I argue that control is an illusion. Looking at these statements from a rational perspective would lead one to determine that this is a paradox. I would not deny that. Many of the things we deal with in social engagement are paradoxical. For example, in order to achieve a degree of control, one needs to let go. According to Poole and van de Ven, we have a decision to make in dealing with such paradoxes. They offer four ways to deal with the problem:

1. Opposition – Accept the paradox and use it constructively, i.e., note the differences and how they influence practices.
2. Spatial separation – using levels of analysis to show where each of the contradictions applies (e.g., behaviors that work for some decision-makers will not work for line staff)
3. Temporal separation – show how opposing phenomena occur at different times. Things that work at some points will not work in others.
4. Synthesis – introduce a new term to resolve the contradict-tion. This draws on the dialectic process as we saw in the Second Wave Positive Psychology material.

This is another explanation of how we must be comfortable with ambiguity. We don't always have clear answers or strategies. Some-times, we just have to allow things to play out. This can be very helpful in framing how we can organize. According to Kabigting, using paradox can breathe life into an organization, making it far more human than the Rational models:

Using the paradoxical mindset can help advance [Second Wave Positive Psychology's] ultimate goal of optimal human functioning, flourishing, and well-being through the recognition and harnessing of the dialectic nature and tendencies of people, organizations, and society.

The idea is that through processing a paradox or contradiction, the group takes responsibility for developing responses or norms. Kabigting further suggests that through this responsibility, the team develops a unifying principle or master virtue (this is related to Aristotle's virtue ethics = phronesis. At this point, this may all seem way too abstract. It is something that is possible, though. What it all means is that we can organize differently. This concept of phronesis is extremely important:

Phronesis is the experiential knowledge that enables people to make ethically sound judgments, enabling leaders to know 'what to do and how to do it, at the right time and with the right people, with the right mix of persuasion and challenge…[it] is knowing which facts and theories matter, when to use which skills, and who should perform actions.

Shapiro describes in some detail how this kind of organizing creates more effective teams and advances the organization's interests. A significant aspect of this form is the development of trust throughout the organization. He points to a real-life organization that applied these concepts. The end result was an organization where learning and trust were the highest values.

T-CVI (Trust-Creating Vulnerable Involvement) practicing PTLers (Phronetic Transforming Leaders) risked their authority as integral to high-moral trustworthy PTL (Phronetic Transforming Leadership) with no expectations for tangible rewards, expecting only intangible ones, in accord with Burns (1978) insistence on the high morality of transformative leaders.

… A major reason the PTLers studied risked their authority by T-CVI was that this risk was minor vis-à-vis the high-moral Pioneering risks they took in the past …

One of the key practices was that the leadership trusted those who did the front-line work to make decisions, not just for the technical practices but also the ethical ones. This is just one example of how a post-rational organization can work. The leadership recognized that different skills and experiences need to be considered and allowed to act as prompts for transformation.

People do not need to be miserable in their jobs. That is the real bottom line here. We need to return the human to human organizations.

Post-traditional governance practice should be an art, where the artistry turns toward the truly human. By truly human, I mean where each and every individual is treated in her fullest human dimension (psycho, socio, bio, spiritual, and other dimensions)—treated as if each person were an artist in the conduct of her own life. Post-traditional practice should be more like an art with this human aim, where practitioners carry out their activities as if they were each creating a work of art

Since technology can take on the drudgery of much of the work that is done in organizations, more people need to be free to be creative problem solvers. We no longer need to discourage relationship building but encourage it. This requires increasing levels of trust and letting go of the need for certainty. I realize that there are circumstances where decisions have serious impacts. In those situations, some care needs to be taken and moral responsibilities assumed. However, I do not believe that these are the majority of conditions. We are all responsible for our growth and development as well as that for the people around us. So, the answer is: We do have to work together, and we do have to be friends. Escaping the Iron Cage of Rationality allows us to do just that.

References

Adam A. Kay, D. P. (2020). Cultivating a conflict-positive workplace: How mindfulness facilitates constructive conflict management. Organizational Behavior and Human Decision Processes, 159, 8-20. Retrieved from

https://doi.org/10.1016/j.obhdp.2020.02.005

Anisha Rajan, M. K. (2026). Effects of mindfulness-based interventions on perceived stress among non-clinical adults: a systematic review and meta-analysis. Mental Health Research, 5(9), 1-9. Retrieved from https://doi.org/10.1038/s44184-026-00188-4

Bandura, A. (1982). Self-Efficacy Mechanism in Human Agency. American Psychology, 37(2), 122-147.

Deann Ladkin, C. S. (2016). The journey of individuation: A Jungian alternative to the theory and practice of leading authentically. Leadership, 1-20.

Farshad Ghasemi, D. Q. (2024). Stress and stress responses: A narrative literature review from physiologicl mechanisms to intervention approaches. Journal of Pacific Rim Psychology, 18, 1-20. doi:10.1177/18344909241289222

Farmer, D. J. (2005). To Kill The King: Post-Traditional Governance and Bureaucracy. Armonk, NY: M. E. Sharpe.

Gigliotti, B. D. (2016). Leadership as Social Influence: An Expanded View of Leadership Communication Theory and Practice. Journal of Leadership & Organizational Studies, 1-13.

Grant, A. (2021). Think Again: The Power of Knowing What You Don't Know. New York: Viking.

Hafenbreck, A. C. (2017). Mindfulness Meditation as an On-The-Spot Workplace Intervention. Journal of Business Research, 118-129.

Houston, E. (2024, August 22). Positive Relationships. Retrieved from positivepsychology.com:

https://positivepsychology.com/positive-relatinship-workplace

Kabat-Zinn, J. (1990). Full catastrophe living. New York: Delacorte.

Kathleen M. Sutcliffe, T. J. (2016). Mindfulness in Organizations: A Cross-Level Review. The Annual Review of Organizational Psychology and Organizational Behavior, 3, 55-81. doi:10.1146/annurev-orgpsych-041015-062531

Kabigting, J. (2022). Responsibility: Enabling Human Consciousness and Flourishing Using Paradox Theory and Existential Positive Psychology (PP 2.o). International Journal of Existential Positive Psychology, 11(1), 1-7.

Morganne A. Kraines, A. E. (2025). Trait Mindfulness and Anxiety Symptoms: The Role of Optimism and Hope. Mindfulness, 16(1), 257-262. Retrieved from https://doi.org/10.1007/s12671-024-02498-0

Qianguo Xiao, C. Y.-y. (2017). The Mindful Self: A mindfulness-Enlightened Self-View. Frontiers in Psychology, 8, 1-10. doi:10.3389/fpsyg.2017.01752

Shapira, R. (2021). Phronetic Leadership: Risking Managerial Authority by Trust-Creating Vulnerable Involvement. Academia Letters. doi:10.20935/AL3336

Theresa M. Glomb, M. K. (2011). Mindfulness at Work. Research in Personnel and Human Resources Management, 30, 115-157.

Uhl-Bien, M. (2006). Relational Leadership Theory: Exploring the social processes of leadership and organizing. The Leadership Quarterly, 17(6), 654-676. Retrieved from

https://doi.org/10.1016/j.leaqua.2006.30.007

Verhaeghen, J. T. (2022). Mind full of kindnes: self-awareness, self-regulation, and self-transcendence as vehicles for compassion. BMC Psychology, 10(188), 1-14. Retrieved from

https://doi.org/10.1186/s40359-022-00888-4

Vincent Kim Seng Oh, A. S. (2022). The study of mindfulness as an intervening factor for enhanced psychological well-being in building the level of resilience. Frontiers in Psychology, 13. Retrieved from https://doi.org.3389/fpsyg.2022.105384

Ven, M. S. (1989). Using Paradox to Build Management and Organization Theories. The Academy of Management Review, 14(4), 562-578. Retrieved from https://doi.org/10.2307/258559

Vlado Dimovsk, M. F. (2012). Authentic Leadership to the Future. Skola biznisa, 1. doi:10.5937/skolbiz1201001D

Warner, C. T. (2019). Self-Betrayal and the Crisis of Self-misunderstanding. Farmington, UT: The Arbinger Institute.

Wendy Kersemackers, S. R. (2018). A workplace Mindfulness Intervention May be Associated with Improved Psychological Well-Being and Productivity: A Preliminary Field Study in a Company Setting. Frontiers in Psychology, 9(195). doi:10.3389/fpsyg.2018.00195

(n.d.).

(ed.), S. v. (2018). The Polemics of Ressentement. London: Bloomsbury Academic.

Aguas, J. J. (2024, September). Martin Bubert's Philosophical Anthropology and Philosophy of Dialogue (First of Two Parts). Kritke, 1-18.

Amanda J. Hancock, I. R. (2023, February). Good, Bad, and Ugly Leadership Patterns: Implications for Followers' Work-Related and Context-Free Outcomes. Journal of Management, 49(2), 640-676. doi:10.1177/01492063211050391

Arbinger Institute. (2018). Leadership and Self-Deception: Getting Out of box. Oakland, CA: Berrett-Koehler Publishing.

Aupperle, W. a. (1984). Bureaucracy as Organizational Pathology. Systems Research, 1(3), 157-166.

Avolio, F. L. (2003). Authentic Leadership Development. In J. E. Kim, S. Cameron, Positive Organizational Scholarship (pp. 241-261). Oakland, CA: Berrett-Koehler.

Baehr, P. (2001). The "Iron Cage" and the "Shell as Hard as Steel": Parsons, Weber, and the Stahlhartes Gehause Metaphor in the Protestant Ethic and the Spirit of Capitalism. History and Theory, 40(2), 153-169. doi:10.1111/0018-2656.00160

Balcomb, A. (2021). Resentment -- Excavating a Resurgent Phenomenon in Contemporary Society. Scriptura, 120(1), 1-15.

Bardach, E. (2017). Networks, Hierarchies, and Hybrids. International Public Management Journal, 20(4), 560-585. doi:10.1080/10967494.2015.1127863

Bauman, Z. (2001). The Individualized Society. Malden, MA: Blackwell Publishers.

Bengtsson, J. O. (1997). Forgotten Roots of Individualism. Humanitas, X(2), 85-95.

Bernstein, J. H. (2009). The Data-Information-Knowledge-Wisdom Hierarchy and its Antithesis. Proceedings North American Symposium on Knowledge Organization, 2, 68-75.

Bravata DM, W. S. (2020, April). Prevalence, Predictors, and Treatment of Impostor Syndrome: a Systematic Review. Journal of General Internal Medicine, 35(4), 1252-1275. doi:10.1007/s11606-019-05364-1

Brown, B. (2017). Braving the Wilderness. New York: Random House.

Buber, M. (1970). I and Thou. Trans. Walter Kaufmann. New York: Simon & Schuster.

Burns, W. (2017, July). A Descriptive Literature Review of Harmful Leadership Styles: Definitions, Commonalities, Measurements, Negative Impacts, and Ways to Improve These Harmful Leadership Styles. Creighton Journal of Interdisciplinary Leadership, 3(1), 33-52.

doi:http://dx.doi.org/10.17062/CJIL.v3i1.53

C.. Terry Warner. (2019). Sel-Betrayal and the Crisis of Self-Misunderstanding. Farmington, Utah: Arbinger Institute.

Calalini, B. (2019). Care of the Self and Subjectivity in Precarious Neoliberal Societies. Insights of Anthropology, 3(1), 134-139.

Caron, F. (2013). Managing the Continuum: Certainty, Uncertainty, Unpredictability in Large Engineering Projects. New York: Springer.

Catherine A. Helmuth, M. S. (2024). Actions are authentic, but are leaders? A reconceptualization of authenticity and leadership practice. Journal of Organizational Behavior, 45, 119-135. doi:10.1002/job. 2723

Christopher J. Soto, J. J. (2020). Five-Factor Model of Personality. New York, UK: Oxford University Press.

doi:10.1093/obo/9780199828340-0120

Clarke, J. (2010, December 22). Embracing Change. Perth, Australia.

Cohen, M. D. (1972, March). A Garbage Can Model of Organizational Choice. Administrative Science Quarterly, 17(1), 1-25. Retrieved from https://doi.org/10.2307/2392088

Columbia University Office of Student Support. (n.d.). The Eisenhower Matrix. Retrieved February 2025, from sps.columbia.edu/sites/default/files/2023-08/Eisenhower%20Matrix.pdf

Coughlin, B. K. (2014). Performance Driven Leadership. Morgan James White Papers.

Cross, S. R. (2024). Micromanagement and its impact on millennial followership styles. Leadership & Organizational Development, 45(1), 140-152. doi:10.1108/LODJ-07-2022-0329

Demircioglu, M. A. (2017). The Effects of Empowerment Practices on Perceived Barriers to Innovation: Evidence from Public Organizations. International Journal of Public Administration. doi:10.1080/01900692.2017

Demircioglu, M. A. (2017). The Effects of Empowerment Practices on Perceived Barriers to Innovation: Evidence from Public Organizations. International Journal of Public Administration. doi:10.1080/01900692.2017.1387143

DiGangi, J. (2023). The Anxious Micromanager. Harvard Business Review.

Donna Ladkin, C. S. (2016). The journey of individuation: A Jungian alternative to the theory and practice of leading authentically. Leadership, 1-20. doi:10.1177/1742715016681942

Dunning, J. K. (1999). Unskilled and Unaware of It: How Difficulties in Recognizing One's Own Incompetence Lead to

Inflated Self-Assessments. Journal of Personality and Social Psychology, 77, 1121-34.

Edgar, P. B. (2011). Rational Gridlock. Lanham, MD: University Press of America.

Finley, A. (2021). How College Contributes to Workforce Success: Employer Views on What Matters Most. Hanover Research. Retrieved August 27, 2025, from

https://www.grinnell.edu/sites/default/files/docs/2025-08/AACUEmployerReport2021.pdf

Fleetwood, S. (2008). Institutions and social structures. Journal for the Theory of Social Behavior, 38(3), 241-265. Retrieved from http://dx.doi.org/10.1111/j.1468?5914.2008.00370.x

Friedman, H. H. (2025, April 16). The education irony: when college degrees lead to unemployment, mindless thinking, debt, and despair. (U. Halreich, Ed.) Academia Mental Health and Well-Being, 1-10. doi:https://doi.org/10.20935/MHealthWellB7661

Galeotti, A. E. (2012). Self-Deception: Intentional Plan or Mental Event. Humana Mente, 41-64.

Gardner, H. (1983). Frames of Mind. New York: Basic Books.

Gavrol, D. (2021). Institutionalism -- A different perception of human behavior and social organization. Academia Letters. Retrieved from https://doi.org/10.20935/AL1632

Gibson, S. G. (2007). Why Does Affect Matter in Organizations? Academy of Management Perspectives, 36-59.

Gigliotti, B. D. (2016). Leadership as Social Influence: An Expanded View of Leadership Communication Theory and Practice. Journal of Leadership & Organizational Studies, 1-13. doi:10.1177/1548051816641876

Goldhaber, G. M. (1986). Organizational Communication (Fourth Edition). Dubuque, Iowa: Wm. C. Brown Publishers.

Goleman, D. (1998). Working with Emotional Intelligence. New York: Bantam Books.

Goleman, D. (1998). Working with Emotional Intelligence. New York: Bantam Books.

Graeme Mitchell, A. J. (2024). Workplace and workplace leader arrogance: A conceptual framework. International Journal of Management Reviews, 26, 608-627. doi:10.1111/ijmr.12372

Grange, L. l. (2017). The University in a Contemporary Era. Higher Education in South Africa, 103-119.

doi:10.188820/9781920338183/06

Grant, A. (2021). Think Again. New York: Viking.

Grant, A. (2021). Think Again. New York: Viking.

Gray, B. (2017). The Cynefin Framework: applying an understanding of complexity to medicine. Journal of Primary Healthcare, 9(4), 258-261. doi:10.1071/HCI7002

Hannes, L. M. (2012). Authentic Leadership and Behavioral Integrity as Drivers of Follower Commitment and Performance. Journal of Business Ethics, 107, 255-264. Retrieved from https://doi.org/10.1007/s10551-011-1036-1

Hayes, D. (2019, November 27). How the University Lost Its Way: Sixteen Threats to Academic Freedom. Postdigital Science and Education. Retrieved from https://doi.org/10.1007/s42438-019-00079-2

Herzberg, F. (1966). Work and the nature of man. Cleveland: World Publishing Co.

Herzberg, F. (1984, November). Mystery Systems Shape Loyalties. Industry Week, 101-104.

Hudson, S. (2010). Intersubjectivity of Mutual Recognition and the I-Thou: a Comparative Analysis of Hegel and Buber. Minerva - An Internet Journal of Philosophy, 140-155.

Hummel, R. P. (2007). The Bureaucratic Experience (5th ed.). Oxfordshire,, England, UK: Routledge.

Iain S. Stewart, V. H. (2022). Editorial: Re-Purposing Universities for Sustainable Human Progress. Frontiers in Sustainability, 1-4. doi:10.3389/frsus.2022.859393

Ibarra, H. (2014, December). The Authenticity Paradox. Harvard Business Review.

Ingrid Smithey Fulmer, B. G. (2023). Compensation and performance: A review and recommendations for the future. Personnel Psychology, 76, 687-717. doi:10.1111/peps 12583

James, W. (2024). K-12 Education: Transforming Public Education for a Changing World. Center for American Progress. Retrieved from https://www.americanprogress.org/article/a-progressive-vision-for-education-in-the-21st-century/k-12-education-transforming-for-a-changing-world

Jesus de la Fuente, J. M. (2022, July). Advances on Self-Regulation Models: A New Research Agenda Through the SR vs ER Behavior Theory in Different Psychology Contexts. Frontiers in Psychology, 13, 1-16. doi:10.3389/psyg. 2022.861493

John T. Wixted, L. M. (2018). Rethinking the Reliability of Eyewitness Memory. Perspectives on Psychological Science, 13(3), 324-335. doi:10.1177/1745691617734878

Julie A. Chesley, T. E. (2020, October). Elevating Leadership Practices to meet Emerging Needs. Journal of Educational Leadership.

Julie A. Shesley, T. E. (2020). Elevating Leadership Development Practices to Meet Emerging Needs. Journal of Leadership Education, 180-191. doi:10.12806/V19/14/T3

Jürgen Mihm, C. H. (2010, May). Hierarchical Structure and Search in Complex Organizations. Management Science, 56(5), 831-848.

Kamenetz, A. (2018). What 'A Nation at Risk' Got Wrong, And Right, About U. S. Schools. NPR. Retrieved from https://www.npr.org/sections/ed/2018/04/29/604986823/

Katz, D. A. (1966). The Social Psychology of Organizations. New York: John Wiley and Sons.

Kernis, M. &. (2006). A multi-component conceptualization of authenticity: Theory and research. In M. P. (ed.), Advances in experimental social psychology (pp. 284-357). Academic Press. Retrieved from https://doi.org/10.1016/S0065-2601(06)38006-9

Killmann, R. H. (2023). Mastering the Thomas-Kilmann Conflict Mode Instrument. Newport Coast, CA: Killman Diagnostics.

Kilmann, R. H. (2023). Mastering the Thomas-Kilmann Conflict Mode Instrument. Newport Coast, CA: Kilmann Diagnostics.

Kolbe, K. (1993). Pure Instinct: The M.O. of High Performance People and Teams. Phoenix, AZ: Momentus Press.

Kolbe, K. (2004). Powered by Instinct: 5 Rules for Trusting Your Guts. Phoenix, AZ: Monumentus Press.

Kolbe, K. (2004). Pure Instinct: The M. O. of High Performance People and Teams. Phoenix: Momentus Press.

Kolbe, K. (2004). Pure Instinct: the M.O. of High Performance People and Teams (2nd ed.). Phoenix, Arizona: Monumentus Press.

Kuhn, T. S. (1996). The Structure of Scientific Revolutions (3rd ed). Chicago: University of Chicago Press.

Lucas Mnzani, P. R. (2014). The moderator role of followers' personality traits in the relations between leadership styles, two types of task performance and work result satisfaction. European Journal of Work and Organizational Psychology.

doi:10.1080/1359432X.2014.911173

Lucas Monzani, P. R. (2014). The moderator role of followers' personality traits in the relations between leadership styles, two types of task performance and work satisfaction. European Journal of Work and Organizational Psychology.

doi:10.1080/1359432X.2014.911173

Lucas Monzani, S. B. (2016). It takes two to tango: The interactive effect of authentic leadership and organizational identification on employee silence intentions. Zeitschrift fur Personalforschung, 30, 246-266. doi:10.1177/2397002216649896

Lynch, K. (2013). Self-deception and shifts of attention. Philosophical Explorations, 17(1), 63-75.

doi:https://doi.org/10.1080/13869795.2013.824109

Maltz, M. (1960). Psycho-cybernetics. New York: Simon & Schuster.

Maslow, A. (1943). A Theory of Human Motivation. Psychological Review, 370-396.

Maslow, A. (1943). A Theory of Human Motivation. Psychological Review, 50, 370-396.

Matej Cerne, V. D. (2014). Congruence of leader self-perception of authentic leadership: Understanding what authentic leadership is and how it enhances employees' job satisfaction. Australian

Journal of Management, 39, 453-471.
doi:10.1177/0312896213503665

Maxwell, N. (2021). How Universities Have Betrayed Reason and
Humanity--And What's to Be Done About it. Frontiers in
Sustainability. Retrieved August 29, 2025, from

https://www.frontiersin.org/research-topics/14778/re-purposing-
universities-for-sustainable-human-progress/magazine?page=2

Maxwell, N. (2021562*564). Universities Betray Reason and, as a
Result, Betray Humanity. Journal of Anthropological and
Archeological Sciences. doi:10.32474/JAAS.2021.04.000199

McClellan, E. F. (2019). The Higher Education "Crisis" and
Political Science. Journal of Political Science Education.
doi:https://doi.org/1080/15512169.2019.1588127

Mele, A. (2001). Self-Deception Unmasked. Princeton: Princeton
Monographs in Philosophy.

Mengyun, Q. H. (2020, January). Workplace Bullying, Anxiety,
and Job Performance: Choosing Between "Passive Resistance" or
"Swallowing the Insult"? Frontiers in Psychology, 10, 1-12.

Merrick, A. (2020). "What Renders Our Sores Repugnant":
Reconsidering Nietzsche on Ressentiment. In M. M. Marco
Brusotti, Europena/Supra-European: Cultural Encounters in
Nietzsche's Philosophy (pp. 117-128). Berlin, Boston: Degruyter.

Merton, R. K. (1957). Social Theory and Social Structure. New
York: MacMillan.

Miles, R. (1965). Human Relations or Human Resources. Harvard
Business Review, 148-157.

Miller McPherson, L. S.-L. (2001). Birds of a Feather: Homophily
in Social Networks. Annual Review of Sociology, 27, 415-444.

Milner, J. (2024). The Motivational Micromanager. Organizational Dynamics, 53. Retrieved January 2025, from

https://doi.org/10.116/j.orgdyn.2024.101054

Montgomery, A. (2016, August 3). linkedin. Retrieved from linkedin.com:

https://www.linkedin.com/pulse/dysfunctional-organzation-definition-cure-angela-montgomery-phd/

Moore, M. (2023, January 13). How Transparent Should You Be with Your Team? Harvard Business Review.

Mortimer, S. A. (2025). Becoming authentic: A social conception of the self. The Philosophical Quarterly, 3-22.

Myers, I. B. (1993). Introduction to Type: A Guide to Understanding Your Results on the MBTI Instrument. Sunnyvale, CA: CPP. Inc.

Myers, I. B. (2015). Introduction to Myers-Briggs Type (Seventh Edition). Sunnyvale, California.

Nelson Cowan, E. J. (2019). Foundations of Arrogance: A Broad Survey and Framework for Research. Review of General Psychology, 23(4), 425-443. doi:10.1177/1089268019877138

O'Driscoll, S. G. (2021). Networks not Hierarchy: Expanding Leadership Capacity and Impact in a Complex World. Institute for Contemporary Leadership, 1-12. Retrieved from

https://contemporaryleadership.com/wp-content/uploads/2021/10/Network-Leadership.pdf

Patricia Duarte, N. R. (2021). Authentic Leadership and Improved Individual Performance: Affective Commitment and Individual Creativity's Sequential Mediation. Frontiers in Psychology, 12, 1-11. doi:10.3389/fpsyg.2021.675749

Patrick Howard, C. O. (2019). Leading Educational Change in the 21st Century: Creating Living Schools through Shared Vision and Transformative Governance. Sustainability, 11, 1-13.

doi:10.3390/su11154109

Payne, P. (2014, October 15). 'Facts and data set you free:' Alan Mulally speakes at the PSBJ's Business Journals Live. Puget Sound Business Journal.

Pelletier, K. L. (2010). Leader Toxicity: an empirical invistigation of toxic behavior and rhetoric. Leadership, 6(4), 373-389. doi:https://doi.org/10.1177/1742715010379308

Picken, J. P. (2012, October). Changing Roles :Leadership in the 21 Century. Organizational Dynamics, 18-34.

Pidarit, S. K. (2000). Recognizing Ambivalence: A Multidimensional View of Attitudes Toward an Organizational Change. Academy of Management Review, 25(4), 783-794.

Pink, D. H. (2011). Drive: The Surprising Truth About What Motivates. New York: Riverhead Books.

Psychology Today staff. (n.d.). Psychology Today. Retrieved 2025, from psychologytoday.com:

https://www.psychologytoday.com/us/basic/groupthink

Puck M. Altera, M. L.-W. (20132, February). Radical Authentic Leadership: Co-creating the conditions under which all members of the organization can be authentic. The Leadership Quarterly, 23(1), 118-131. Retrieved from

https://www.sciencedirect.com/science/article/abs/pii/S104898431 1001731?via%3Dihub

Putnam, R. D. (2000). Bowling Alone: The Collapse and Revival of American Comunity. New York: Simon & Schuster.

Qingqing Li, X. R. (2023). Reciprocal relationships between self-control and self-autheticity: a two-wave study. Frontiers in Psychology, 01-07. doi:10.3389/fpsyg.2023.1207230

Raelin, J. (2020, December). In Leadership, Look to the Practices Not to the Individual. Academia Letters. Retrieved from https://doi.org/10.20935/AL34

Raelin, J. (2021). Leadership-as-Practice: Antecedent to Leadersul Purpose. Journal of Change Management.

doi:doi.org10.1080/14697017.2021.1942966

Rohr, R. (2011). Immortal Diamond: The Search for Our True Self. Hoboken, NJ: Jossey-Bass.

Salazar, M. (2017). "Let's be clear": Exploring the Role of Transparency Within the Organization. Cornerstone: A Collection of Scholarly and Creative Works for Minnesota State University, Makato. Retrieved from https://cornerstone.lib.mnsu.edu/etds/720/

Samuel Bazzi, M. F. (2020, November). Frontier Culture: The Roots and Persistence of "Rugged Individualism" in the United States. Econometrica, 88(6), 2329-2368.

Schwartz SH, M. G. (2001). Extending the cross-cultural validity of the theory of basic human values witha different method of measurement. Journal of Cross-Cultural Psychology, 519-42.

Simon, H. (1957). Administrative Behavior: A Study of Decision-Making (second editin). New York: MacMillan.

Simon, H. (1957). Administrative Behavior: A Study of Decision-Making Processes in Administrative Organization, second edition. New York: MacMillan.

Sinek, S. (2025). Start with Why 15th Anniversary Edition: How Great Leaders Inspire Everyone to Take Action. New York: Portfolio.

Smith, D. L. (2014). Self-Deception: A Teleofunctional Approach. Philosophia, 42(1), 181-199.

Smith, J. H. (1987, March). Elton Mayo and the Hidden Hawthorne. Work, Employment & Society, 1(1), 107-120.

Snowden, D. J. (2007). A Leader's Framework for Decision Making. Harvard Business Review, 85(11), 68-76.

Soniya Billore, T. A. (2023). Sel-regulation and goal-directed behavior: A systematic literature review, public policy recommendations, and research agenda. Journal of Business Research, 156, 1-19. Retrieved from

https://doi.org/10.1016/j.jbusres.20223113435

Sorensen, E. a. (2024, May 16). The ideational robustness of bureaucracy. Policy and Society, 43(2), 141-158.

doi:https://doi.org/10.1093/polsoc/puae015

Stanley B. Silverman, R. E. (2012). Arrogance: A Formula for Leadership Failure. The Industrial-Organizational Psychologist, 50(1), 21-28.

Steven M. Normnan, B. J. (2010). The impact of positivity and transparency on trust in leaders and their perceived effectiveness. The Leadership Quarterly, 21, 350-364.

doi:10.1016/j.leaqua.2010.03.002

Sun, M. H. (2017). Reviewing Leadership Styles Overlaps and the Need for a New 'Full Range' Theory. International Journal of Management Reviews, 19, 76-96.

Taylor, F. W. (1911). The Principles of Scientific Management. New York: Harper Brothers.

Taylor, F. W. (1911). The Principles of Scientific Management. New York: Harper & Brothers.

TedxUSU (Producer). (2016). The Beauty of Conflict [Motion Picture]. Retrieved from youtube.com/watch?v=55n9pH_A008

The Enneagram Institute. (2026). enneagraminstitute.com. Retrieved February 2026, from The Enneagram Institute: https://www.enneagraminstitute.com/

Tolstoy, L. (2004). War and Peace. New York: The Modern Library.

United States National Commission on Excellence in Education. (1983). A Nation at Risk: the imperative for educational reform: A report to the nation and the Secretary of Education. Washington, D.C.: Superintendent of Documents, U. S, Government Printing Office.

Van Eerde, W. &. (1996). Vroom's expectancy models and work-related criteria: A meta-analysis. (5, Ed.) Journal of Applied Psychology, 81, 575-586.

Vugt, M. V. (2006). Evolutionary Origins of Leadership and Followership. Personality and Social Psychlogy Review, 10(4), 354-371.

Walumbwa, F. O. (2008). Authentic Leadership: Development and validation of a theory-based measure. Journal of Management. Retrieved from https://doi.org/10.1177/0149206307308913

Warner, C. T. (2019). Self-Betrayal and the Crisis of Self-Misunderstanding. Farmington, Utah: Arbinger Institute.

Watzlawick, P. B. (2011). Pragmatics of Human Communication: A Study of Interactional Patterns, Pathologies and Paradoxes (Reprint Edition). New York, NY: W. W. Norton.

Weber, M. (1946). Bureaucracy. In M. Weber, Essays in Sociology (editied and translated by H. H. Gerth and C. Wright Mills. Oxford: Oxford University Press.

Weber, M. (1946). Essays in Sociology -- translated by Gerth and Mills. New York: Oxford University Press.

Weick, K. E. (1979). The Social Psychology of Organizing. New York: McGraw-Hill.

Weick, K. E. (1993). Collective mind in organizations: heedful interrelating on flight decks. Administrative Science Quarterly, 38, 357-81.

Weick, K. E. (1995). Sensemaking in Organizations. Thousand Oaks, CA: Sage.

Weick, K. S. (2005). Organizing and the Process of Sensemaking. Organization Science, 409-421.

William Gardner, B. A. (2005). "Can you see the real me?" A Self-based model of authentic leader and follower development. The Leadership Quarterly, 16, 343-372.

doi:10.1016/leaqua.2005.03.003

William L. Gardner, B. A. (2005). "Can you see the rel me?" A Self-based model of authentic leader and follower development. The Leadership Quarterly, 343-372. doi:10.1016/j.leaqua.2005.03.003

About The Author:
Patrick B. Sullivan, DPA

Patrick Sullivan is a Navy veteran living in Montana. He received his BA in History/Political Science and Master of Public Administration degrees from the University of Montana, a Master of Divinity degree from the Franciscan School of Theology in Berkeley, CA, and his Doctor of Public Administration from the University of Southern California. He has been a professor at two institutions for 12 years. He has a total of 50 + years of experience in the public and private sectors. Patrick has worked as a consultant in organizational behavior since 1987.

Patrick is also the author of Rational Gridlock under his previous name Patrick B. Edgar.

Patrick is the father of two; grandfather of seven; and great-grandfather of two.